BECOME A SUPERLEARNER:
LEARN SPEED READING &
ADVANCED MEMORY

BY

JONATHAN LEVI

WITH

LEV GOLDENTOUCH
ANNA GOLDENTOUCH

J. LEVI PUBLISHING

Become a SuperLearner: Learn Speed Reading & Advanced Memory

ISBN-13:978-0692416952
ISBN-10:0692416951

Never Stop Learning!

To my loving parents and godparents, who taught me to value learning, knowledge, and self-improvement above all else.

FOREWORD

I became a SuperLearner by accident in 2008.

I had just taken a year sabbatical from grad school and moved to Chicago to chase a girl (which was a horrible idea given the fact that it was right at the front of the recession), and I was having some serious trouble finding a quality job. Story short, I ended up waiting tables for a year.

In the process of finding work, I had a lot of free time on my hands. A lot of it was spent applying to jobs, but the rest was spent on a couch reading. It started with books about the brain. How memory worked, what memory was, how we perceive things, why we perceive things, names and descriptions of parts of the brain, neurological diseases and disorders – the whole gamut. You see, my grandmother was in very advanced stages of Alzheimer's, which kept me constantly with her memory on my mind.

That eventually led me to investigate curious anecdotes of curious people with curious brains. The most famous one being Kim Peek (the inspiration for the 1988 film, *Rainman*), an autistic savant who was able to read and memorize two pages of books at a time or count the amount of dropped toothpicks in seconds. Less famous were people like Rüdiger Gamm, a mental calculation prodigy who could calculate any 2-digit number's power (provided the power was a low-ish number), and Ben Pridmore, one of the best competitive memorizers in the world and the at-the-time world record holder for memorizing a deck of cards (in 24.74 seconds!).

The fascinating thing about these latter "savants," was that they were actually just ordinary people (or at least they claimed to be). They claimed to have taught and trained themselves those mind-bending abilities. Ben and his memory fascinated me simply because I had always had a poor memory and absolutely refused to believe it was a thing I could just train and turn on. Because of my grandmother's increasingly failing memory, I was especially interested in improving my memory.

I spent the next few months trying to learn as much as I could, but it was a tricky thing trying to find all of the information in one place. I would find an out-of-date book about this technique over here, that failed to mention an even better technique for that over there, and the rest was all scattered over the internet. I remember it being very frustrating. Back then, and pretty much still to this day, there have not been any books that really smash it out of the park with having all the right techniques and tools in one place. Thankfully, *SuperLearning* does. The authors of this book have concentrated, condensed, and made easily digestible all the things you need to be a well-rounded Super Learner, all into one book. I seriously wish I had had this book back when I started.

But now *you* do.

Fast forward a year after I started learning Super Learning techniques, my grandmother passes away and I move back home to Miami to finish grad school. Her passing gives me motivation and inspiration like I have never felt and I end up taking my memory skills to the next level. Long story short, I ended up winning the championship 3 times between 2010 and 2014, but I developed skills that changed my brain for my entire life. As a result of SuperLearning, I have changed the way I live my life and approach absolutely everything. It was the single most important addition to my life.

Now it's your turn!

Nelson Dellis
4-Time USA Memory Games Champion
March 2015

PREFACE

"What you have in your pocket, anyone can take. What you have in your mind, nobody can."

-Unknown

This course was developed out of a deep passion for personal development and a sincere desire to help others learn more effectively. By the end of this course, you will improve your memory, learn the skills to increase your reading speed, and increase your comprehension. In short, you will become a SuperLearner.

What is a "SuperLearner"? A SuperLearner is a person who has a deep and burning thirst for vast amounts of knowledge, and the means, skills, and habits to acquire that knowledge rapidly. A SuperLearner simply seeks to push beyond the boundaries of traditional, laborious learning, and add skillsets to his or her life that vastly improve their effectiveness in our information-driven world.

The skills, methods and techniques taught in this course have helped tens of thousands of students increase their reading speed, "hack" their learning process, and develop the infrastructure for remembering an influx new information. Though originally offered as a bestselling online course, the material has been meticulously and lovingly adapted for both paperback and eBook formats.

As Jonathan walks the reader through the process of becoming a SuperLearner, he refers to the currently popular idea of "life hacking." *Wikipedia* defines "life hacking" as follows:

> **Life hacking** refers to any trick, shortcut, skill, or novelty method that increases productivity and efficiency, in all walks of life. It is arguably a modern appropriation of a Gordian knot - in other words, anything that solves an everyday problem

in an inspired, ingenious manner. (Ref: http://jle.vi/gc)

Terminology changes from generation to generation. However, the ability to become a SuperLearner is irrespective of age or generational terminology. Whether you are seeking to "hack" a solution, "learn" a new skill, "develop" a new habit, "ace" the ability to learn, or "keep" your mind sharp, this course will guide you through the steps necessary to accomplish your goal. If your goal is to be able to read faster with greater comprehension and set up a structured system for accessing the information you learn, then this course will help you obtain those goals.

The course lays out progressive steps with each section introducing new skills, which build upon the previous section. There are homework assignments and quizzes in each section. The homework provides the necessary practice to develop the skills of a SuperLearner.

Therefore, it is vitally important that you progress through each section in the order presented. If you skip around, you may very well become frustrated and miss the ultimate skill of becoming a true SuperLearner.

TABLE OF CONTENTS

SECTION 1: INTRODUCTION TO THE COURSE

CHAPTER 1: HOW THIS COURSE CAME TO BE

My name is Jonathan Levi. I have the distinct privilege and honor to explain the skills taught in this course. Along the way, you will learn how to develop those skills to become a SuperLearner.

My friends and coauthors, Dr. Lev Goldentouch and Prof. Anna Goldentouch, answer common questions from current and former students in the "Ask Dr. Lev" and "Ask Prof. Anna" sections in various chapters. We each are excited to offer this course, to help you become a SuperLearner, and to open doors that enhance your lifestyle. If you have additional questions, please feel free to use the links in the PDF Syllabus to contact myself, Dr. Lev (via the *KeyToStudy* blog), or to post in the course *Facebook* Group.

WE BEGIN WITH A STORY...

Before we get started, I would like to tell you a quick story of how this course actually came to be. Several years ago, I was working in a venture capital firm with some very smart people. I came to know Lev Goldentouch who was working in one of the startups in the firm.

Lev and I started to talk. Before long, we started sending each other articles from *TechCrunch* or *Psychology Today*. We had many similar interests.

However, I noticed something interesting. When I would send Lev an article, I would get a reply back in about a minute or two with half a page of comments. Lev also had a habit of sending me five to ten news articles every morning as he sat there and drank his coffee. These articles were often sent about a minute or two apart and all came in the span of under half an hour.

Eventually, I started to wonder what was up, and so I went into Lev's office. I saw him scrolling up and down on the page. I said, "Lev, if you are not actually going to read the article, just tell me you are not interested and that is fine, I will stop sending them." Lev told me, "Actually, I did read the article."

When I looked into his comments, I saw that, in fact, his comprehension of the article was extraordinarily high. I said, "Oh, you read the article before I sent it to you." However, I was mistaken. I saw Lev scrolling rapidly on a page as we chatted, and continued my line of inquiry: "So, you're scrolling through and skimming the articles?" Lev replied, "No, the speed at which I scroll is actually the speed of me reading."

I was shocked. I immediately scoffed, "How's that possible? How do you have that level of detail and clarity when you are scrolling on the page as fast as I would scroll if I were searching for something?" Lev told me that his wife, Anna, is one of the leading specialists here in Israel in the field of speed reading and SuperLearning. I am a big believer in kismet, and on that day, it was working in my favor.

I had previously tried to learn the skill of speed reading and, quite frankly, never succeeded. I tried Tim Ferriss' *PX Method*, and the Evelyn Wood's *Seven-Day Speed Reading and Learning Program*. I learned to scan and turn pages very quickly, but my comprehension was appalling.

When Lev and I checked, my speed was actually about 450 words a minute, with 20 to 30% comprehension. Lev, on the other hand, was comfortably reading about 1200 words a minute - at 80 to 90% comprehension. The difference was dramatic. Lev was able to read a 300-page book in about an hour and a half, tell me *all* the pertinent details, and where to find everything.

I have always been interested in accelerated learning and life hacking. In fact, I was on my way to a condensed ten-month MBA program, where I would have a ton of reading and a ton of stress.

Lev generously offered to introduce me to his wife for one-on-one training sessions. I took Anna's course, (which was *not* cheap, by the way) and it took about six weeks. Those six weeks changed my life more than I could have ever imagined.

In the process of obtaining my MBA, I would find myself reading the pages of an exam and then looking up to rest my eyes as I planned about my response. Without fail, everyone else in the auditorium would take another 10 to 15 minutes to read the exact same content.

There were many funny times where study group mates would comment, "You know, we'd appreciate it if you would actually read the article." I echoed Lev's words to me earlier, "I read the article. Check out page 32, Exhibit C. You will find the exact information you've been looking for."

No "Genius" Designation Required

It is very important to note that Lev, his wife Anna, and I are not particularly genius people. However, we each were taught to learn quickly and effectively. We have learned to take advantage of the things that our brains are most drawn to, and we are now able use that understanding to accelerate our learning and understanding.

Now, ever since I acquired this skill, I have had many people ask me how they too can learn to do the same thing. I have shared Anna's course with a number of people. In fact, a few of my friends have taken it, either in person or on Skype. However, Anna is only one woman, and a mother of three at that, and, as I mentioned, her course is not cheap.

That was the beginning of the brainstorming sessions. Anna, Lev and I wanted a way that we could share this incredible skill set with the world.

I was taking some courses online, including one on *Udemy*, and I thought it would be a great platform to teach this skillset to many people. Anna's course had never been recorded, and other than one-on-one Skype sessions, had never been taught online before. Lev, Anna, and I thought it would be a great way to spread the potential of Anna's teachings. We collaborated on the course and result was our bestselling online course on

Udemy. At the time of this publication, we are among the most successful paid courses of all time having enrolled roughly 25,000 students!

Our next goal was to produce this book, so that many others may have the opportunity to become SuperLearners.

LAYING THE GROUNDWORK

You are probably very eager to get started. However, there are a few more things to cover as we lay the groundwork for effective use of this course.

First, at the end of some chapters, there are recommended supplementary materials that are hyperlinked in the PDF Syllabus (see Chapter 2). Pay attention to these resources, as they are an integral part of this course.

HOMEWORK

Download the Syllabus for this course at **http://jle.vi/pdf**.

After you download the Syllabus, check out the recommended supplementary materials for this chapter. The supplementary material is a vital part of this course. As you interact with the material, it will increase your ability achieve your goal of becoming a SuperLearner. More on that later.

CHAPTER 2: COURSE SYLLABUS & PROPOSED TRAINING SCHEDULE

ONLINE RESOURCES

SuperLearner Syllabus: This is an extremely important document because this gives you all the resources that we cover in the course with convenient and easy to find links. Begin by downloading the PDF Syllabus at **http://jle.vi/pdf**. Please note the sections and chapters of this book correspond to the Syllabus. The resource material and exercises are clickable links in the PDF file, and provide much faster access to the online exercises and external resource material utilized in this course.

It is imperative to note that all the exercises and all the supplemental resources are integral parts of this course. The exercises are designed specifically to achieve targeted skills, and fulfill some of the psychological requirements for adult learning. The supplemental resources give you not only practice and improve skill sets, they are also an important part of training your mindset and ensuring your success as you go through the course.

Browser Bookmark ZIP File: If you are tech savvy, you may also choose download the SuperLearner Bookmarks ZIP file (**http://jle.vi/bookmarks**), which you can import into your browser to add instantly all of the resources to your bookmarks.

PROPOSED TRAINING SCHEDULE

"HOW LONG UNTIL I WILL BE ABLE TO…?"

Students love to ask these types of questions, and the answer is always: "*it depends.*"

This outline serves as a rough timeline that will apply to the average student. Of course, every student arrives to the course with different levels of training, different learning challenges, and different bad habits. For this reason, different exercises and milestones will take longer for different people.

In each step, we try to provide an indication as to when you will know it's time move on. There is a suggestion along the side of the PDF Syllabus as to *roughly* where you should be each week.

Please note the Syllabus has been included below in a slightly different format. As always, use your judgement. If you need more time to master an exercise, then spend the time to accomplish your goal. Do not force yourself to move on just meet an arbitrary timeline. Because adult learners all have different schedules and responsibilities, the dedicated time for learning new skills may not be conducive to the schedule provided. Remember, it is a guideline.

REMEMBER: LEARNING IS NOT A SPECTATOR SPORT!

WEEK 1

SECTION 1: INTRODUCTION

Chapter 1   About Us: How This Course Came To Be

Chapter 2   Course Syllabus

Chapter 3   Learning How To Learn

Chapter 4   What is a "Super Learner," Anyways?

Chapter 5   Overview: What You Will Be Learning

SECTION 2: IMPROVE YOUR MEMORY: BUILDING THE SUPERLEARNING INFRASTRUCTURE

Chapter 6   Why We Need To Improve Our Memory First

Chapter 7   How We Store Information: A Very Brief Explanation

Chapter 8   Why Images Are The Most Powerful Way To Remember

Chapter 9   What Types Of Images Come Naturally To You?

Chapter 10   The Theory In Action: Learning Something New

WEEK 2

SECTION 3: USING MENTAL MARKERS FOR LEARNING

Chapter 11   What Do Pictures Have To Do With Reading?

Chapter 12   Creating Effective Markers For Better Memory

Chapter 13   Demonstration: Creating Markers As We Read

Chapter 14   Trying Out Your New Skills

Chapter 15   Linking Markers For Better Retention

WEEK 3

WEEK 4

WEEK 5

WEEK 6

WEEK 7 AND BEYOND – NEVER QUIT

> ## "ONCE YOU STOP LEARNING, YOU START DYING."
> ## –ALBERT EINSTEIN

AT THE CONCLUSION OF THE SIX WEEKS:

You should also continue to monitor your reading speed and practice the relevant exercises until you reach at least 700 wpm with 85% comprehension. Usually, this happens around week 10.

CLOSING THOUGHT

1. Do something every day. Make the time for *at least* 10 minutes of practice every day.

2. Don't rush through the material. New skills take time to learn and then practice to perfect. You cannot become a concert pianist in six weeks, especially if you do not know how to read the notes on the music in front of you!

HOMEWORK

Check the PDF Syllabus for homework assignments and recommended supplementary materials.

CHAPTER 3: LEARNING HOW TO LEARN

This chapter will explain the necessity of overcoming some deeply ingrained bad habits and crutches in order to unlock our potential as a SuperLearner.

As we dive into the course, we are going to be **re-learning how to learn**. Of course, you have not gotten this far in life without an ability to learn. Yet, no matter where your skill level is for learning, you can benefit from learning these skills. Anyone from a struggling high school student to a skilled musician or top programmer can learn these skills and thereby increase their ability to learn.

Obviously, you know how to read, or you would not have bought this book. Second, you have a desire to increase your reading speed, comprehension, and memory skills in order to become a SuperLearner.

Congratulations!

You already have what it takes to become a SuperLearner. As mentioned earlier, the prerequisites for becoming a SuperLearner are determination, diligence, and learning how to best utilize brain functions.

However, we need to break a lot of the old learning habits and behaviors that have been ingrained in the past. Behaviors like laying in a dark room while reading and studying. Another behavior that is critical to break is the habit of "subvocalization." This and many other habits will be explained as we progress through the course.

TRAINING METHODOLOGY

By design, we are going to be using a training methodology called progressive overload. Weight lifters and bodybuilders use this same methodology. They consistently overload their body's capabilities forcing the body, or in our case, the mind to adapt.

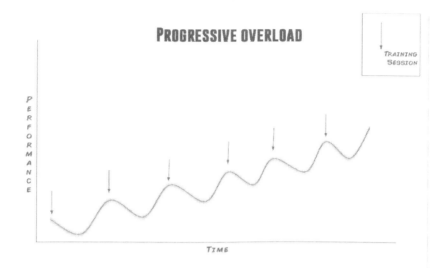

Over time, in a sequence of adaptations, you will see dramatic improvements but that does not mean it is pleasant or easy along the way.

Frustration Is Normal

You are going to confront a lot of resistance as you try to break these old habits, and that is okay. It is part of the process. Just understand that speed reading and accelerated learning can help with a whole host of things, from attention deficit to memory issues.

We are going to get there. Just be patient with yourself. Do not beat yourself up and remember that some of these habits you have had for many years.

These habits are crutches that you have come to rely on. It is perfectly natural to encounter some resistance and difficulty in overcoming them. Do not worry, in time you will learn to walk and even run without those old crutches.

Homework

Check the Syllabus for homework assignments and recommended supplementary materials.

CHAPTER 4: WHAT IS A SUPERLEARNER?

SUPERLEARNER DEFINITION

A SuperLearner is someone who is able to synthesize, understand, and retain vast amounts of information in a short time period.

In this chapter, we will meet some SuperLearners and begin to explore how they function. Check out the videos in the supplementary materials!

> **SuperLearner** (noun): One who is repeatedly able to synthesize, understand, and retain vast amounts of information in abnormally short periods of time.

Now, let's make sure we have clear understanding of what exactly a SuperLearner is. In my mind, a SuperLearner is someone who is able to synthesize, understand, and retain a vast amount of information in a very short timeframe. I was personally first turned on to the idea of SuperLearning when I read Tim Ferriss' *The 4 -Hour Workweek*.

Tim has his own strategy for accelerated learning, which leans heavily on something called the Pareto Principle. It is the idea that 20% of the results come from 80% of the efforts and 80% of the results come from 20% of the efforts. Tim then finds the 20% that is going to yield the 80% and he concentrates his efforts on that 20%. By concentrating on the 20%, he has been able to become a salsa champion, a sumo-wrestling champion, learn languages in short periods of time, and so on.

IMPORTANT:

SuperLearning does not mean that we are sacrificing quality of learning or doing the bare minimum. In fact, other famous SuperLearners include

Elon Musk, the cofounder of PayPal, Inc. and CEO of Tesla Motors, and SpaceX; or how about Tim Doner, a 19 or 20-year old kid who showed up on *YouTube* in May 2013, and has taught himself 23 languages (at various levels) since the age of 13.

In addition, another famous polyglot recently gave a *TED* Talk. His name is Benny Lewis. He has developed a system for fluently speaking a language in just three months. He has learned eight languages so far. He is definitely an amazing SuperLearner.

Make sure to reference the Syllabus for clickable links to the videos of some of these amazing people. One common thread that you will notice with all of them is not one of them claims to be geniuses. Take the time to watch these videos.

SUPERLEARNERS are not exceptional, geniuses, or gifted people. They are people with a desire to learn and unique methods to do so. They are learning *how* to learn.

In fact, the majority of these people say that anyone can do what they do. Benny, for example, struggled for years even to learn Gaeilge, the second language in his home country of Ireland. SuperLearners have trained themselves in various highly effective skills in reading, memory and so on to overcome all the usual challenges of education. With enough work, you will do the same.

HOMEWORK

Check the Syllabus for homework assignments and recommended supplementary materials.

CHAPTER 5: AN OVERVIEW OF WHAT YOU WILL BE LEARNING

CHAPTER OVERVIEW

This chapter will give you an overview into what we will be learning. While you may be excited to dive immediately into a book or an online course you have been meaning to get around to, it is important that we learn the skills in the appropriate order, so you get the most out of this course.

UNDERSTAND THE GOAL

Our goal is to become a SuperLearner. We understand there are old learning habits to break and new skills to learn.

Now, let's talk about how we are going to get there. I want to give you a quick overview of what we are going to be learning and in what order. I know you want to dive in and go as fast as you can. You may be tempted to jump around and try out different chapters in this book just to "see what they are" or "see if they work."

However, and this is a really big however, it is important you learn these skills in the appropriate order, so you get the most out of this course. ***Jumping around will leave you frustrated and, and will not teach you anything.***

First and foremost, in Part 2, we have to work on our memory. We have to gain a general understanding of how new information is learned.

In Part 3, we will start talking about "Mental Markers." This is a hugely important habit for effective learning. We will be spending quite a bit of time perfecting our skills there.

Then in Part 4, pre-reading and prep work, we are going to learn how to prepare our minds for intensive learning sessions with a brief overview of some best practices.

Once all that is done, in Part 5 we are finally ready to learn speed reading. We will be learning the difference between how most people read and how speed readers read. I will actually be teaching you some incredible techniques that will double or triple your reading speed almost instantly, and improve your comprehension and focus. Since we have done the groundwork of improving memory at that point, you will be able to comprehend and retain most of that information. In fact, you will retain much more than you could have ever imagined.

In Part 6, we will speed things up even more, with some hacks to smooth out the learning curve of speed reading.

By Part 7, you will have developed the capacity to absorb huge amounts of information very quickly; we will therefore learn how to store this information long-term.

In Part 8, we address healthy learning habits to give you that extra edge.

Finally, in Part 9, I will teach you how to tailor your new skills towards different things like learning languages, meeting people, absorbing online classes, and much more.

Let me just say, I know it seems like a long journey until we get to the really sexy parts like speed reading; however, *please be patient*. As I said, it is important we take things step by step. This course is not meant to be consumed in a day, a few days, or even a couple of weeks.

Along the way, you should practice the different skills and exercises we are going to give you. Together, these exercises should be practiced 20-60 minutes a day until you see significant progress. Only then should you move on to the next set of exercises. It is fine to read the next set of chapters or section, but *do not rush yourself*.

PRACTICE: 20 to 60 minutes a day until you see significant progress and then move to the next set of exercises

Every skill is going to build on previous skills. It is like building a brick wall. If the foundation is faulty, the wall will crumble. If even one row of bricks is set off center, the wall will not hold in strong winds. Learning the skills in order and learning them well will prepare the foundation for your future learning endeavors and will hold fast in the heat of MBA exams, oral exams or jobs that require tons of reading and recall.

It is better to take an extra day, or even a week, to learn the skills in order to get the most out of the exercises than to push yourself to meet some arbitrary time designation in order to rush through the course. Move forward at your own pace and keep progressing in the learning process. Shoes do not come in just one size. Individuals do not progress at the same rate. It is okay to learn new skills at your pace.

The caveat is to practice daily. The old adage always applies to learning new skills – *use it or lose it.*

ONE LAST THING

Okay, we have just one more very important thing to cover before we get started.

I want you to grab a writing instrument. I want you write down in the space provided below 3 to 5 different goals and/or reasons why you want to become a SuperLearner.

Explain to yourself why this is an important thing for you to acquire and why are you going to put in the work to make it happen. Later on, when we talk a little bit about the requirements for adult learners, you will understand why this was such an important step to complete in advance.

So, go ahead and write those things down. Do not skip this step. It is really extremely important.

My Goals / Reasons For Wanting To Succeed In This Course

1.

2.

3.

4.

5.

ASK DR. LEV: SETTING YOUR SUPERLEARNING GOALS

When you try to develop SuperLearning skills, it is very important not to lose sight of your goals.

Do I want to develop a super-skill? Super-skills set us apart from other human beings, help promote our reputation on LinkedIn and draw people to us in various ways we enjoy. However, this comes with a price. While the word record in speed reading is above 10,000 words per minute, I do not know anyone who actually needs to read THAT fast. I have spent almost 10 years developing my learning skills, and I hold a modest 2000 words per minute position. Jonathan and most of my best students stop around 1000 words per minute. Why? They just cannot afford to read hundreds of articles per week. If you really want to excel, you need to spend at least 1-2 hours per day speed reading. Do you have enough curiosity, time and willingness to read that much?

Do you want to read FAST? Reading at 1000 wpm is very fast. Often other people look at this in disbelief. You could read almost any article in minutes, forming a qualified opinion on almost any subject. This is a proper result of our SuperLearning course done right.

Now the question is how do you keep the speed from dropping? You will start to lose speed if you:

- Do not read at least 15 minutes a day
- Jump from language to language without training in one language consistently
- Do not get enough sleep

Therefore, before you get to 1000 wpm, ask yourself, "What kind of material will I enjoy and can easily obtain that will keep me speed-reading at least 15 minutes a day?"

Do you want to pass exams? If you want to pass exams, the core value of this course is improving your retention and not your reading speed.

- Do spend more time on various ways to make markers and link them together.
- Do spend more time on finding your personal style and on creating stories.

The saccades and subvocalization suppression may be wrong for you right now, since they take weeks to master and even then, they marginally reduce the retention quality.

Do you want to master a field of knowledge? When you are trying to master a new field of knowledge, the ability to links ideas together is more important than the ability to read or remember a piece of information. You should investigate complex ways of chunking data and linking all the pieces of data you have together. You should also prioritize and distinguish what to focus on and what is "nice to have." Most importantly, every time you read something completely new, pause a bit to process the information: creating great links takes time and creative effort.

Do you want it all? Eventually you may read this list and understand that you want it all. This means that you can revisit this book and our online resources from time to time and adapt to the SuperLearning style that is best for you now.

HOMEWORK

Check the Syllabus for homework assignments and recommended supplementary materials.

SECTION 2: IMPROVE YOUR MEMORY: BUILDING THE INFRASTRUCTURE FOR SUPER-LEARNING

Chapter 6: Why We Need To Improve Our Memory First

Chapter Overview

We are going to start our journey by improving our memory. This chapter will explain why that is so important.

Fortunately, this is not boring stuff at all. This is a general theory of how to improve learning, not just for reading, but also for meeting new people, learning new skills, and more. While we work our way through the course, you will be able to apply these skills in your everyday life, and that by itself is an important aspect of learning.

The Hose And Bucket Metaphor

So, let's dive in and start by improving our memory.

To understand why we need to improve our memory first, I want you to imagine a bucket. Above that bucket, you have a funnel and pointing into the bucket right now is your average garden hose. Filling the bucket is no problem, right?

Now, imagine we switch out that garden hose for a fire hose. Big problem, right? The funnel overflows, water spills everywhere. In about a second the bucket overflows, too, and it is not long before you have to shut the water off completely.

If we take this metaphor for our learning process, it is easy to understand why we have to upgrade the bucket first, and then the funnel before we finally upgrade the hose.

> **SuperLearning** is only possible with the proper infrastructure in place.

This is to say that without the right infrastructure, speed reading is useless, even impossible, and that is why I personally failed twice before reaching Anna's course.

As a demonstration of my reading speed, imagine scrolling through a webpage at a constant, steady pace. Now, reading this quickly is actually not nearly as challenging as you might think.

Comprehension (or what we call markers (mental images that have been created)/storing memories) at this speed is a very different challenge. That is why we must improve our memory first.

ROTE MEMORIZATION AND/OR CHILDHOOD MNEMONICS

Most of us, when we have to learn new information, are subjected to rote learning (memorization of information based on repetition) or the mnemonic devices of our childhood, such as, I before E except after C, or the mathematic algorithm, PEMDAS (parentheses, exponents, multiplication/division, addition/subtraction).

These methods are hugely effective for children learning simple things like mathematical conventions, but they do not allow us much flexibility with the information, and we become highly dependent on them. How many of you, for example, have to think back to the alphabet song before you can confidently declare what the 11th letter is in alphabet?

NEW MEMORIZATION SKILLS

What if you were required to memorize:

- Information that is much more complex
- The chronological order of historical events
- All the ligaments in the human body

For those types of learning requirements, you need an entirely new set of memorization skills. You would need skills that give you a richer understanding of material extending way beyond songs or acronyms.

Don't worry; it is actually much more fun than it sounds. This is a general theory on how to improve learning, not just for reading but also for meeting new people, learning new memorization and retention skills, and much more. While we work our way through the course, you will be able to apply these skills in your daily life, and that feeling of success will only accelerate your progress and motivation.

IF YOU DON'T USE IT, YOU LITERALLY LOSE IT!

HOMEWORK

Check the Syllabus for homework assignments and recommended supplementary materials.

CHAPTER 7: HOW WE STORE INFORMATION: A VERY BRIEF EXPLANATION

CHAPTER OVERVIEW

This chapter is extremely crucial. It explains the inner workings of the brain (in layman's terms), and helps us understand how we can "hack" the system our brain uses to record information. No prior knowledge is required, and the supplementary information below is optional, just in case you are curious to learn more!

YOUR BRAIN

Now, I am not a cognitive scientist, and, so you are going to have to forgive this very basic explanation. It is important that you understand why we do some of the strange things that we are going to do in this course, and how this relates to the actual inner workings of your brain.

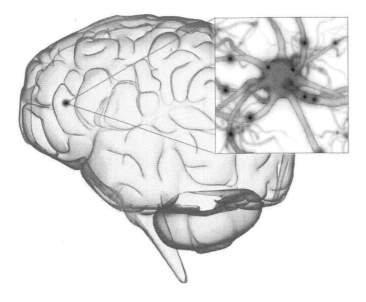

Your brain is made up of tiny little cells called neurons.

These electrically excitable cells process and transmit information using electrochemical signals. These signals are called synapses.

Synapses are specialized connections between the cells, but that is not relevant at this point. What you need to know is that neurons connect to each other, and form neural networks.

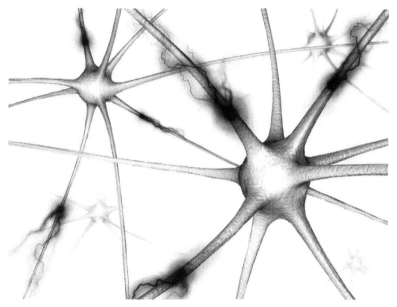

Now this is where it gets **really, really** important.

The more connections there are to a neuron, the less likely it is to be removed or to fade away.

To give you a metaphor, I want you to imagine two roads. One is a six-lane highway connecting eight medium sized towns, and another one is a country road connecting one house to another.

Which road is more likely to receive regular maintenance and improvements? Which road is more likely to be neglected and eroded from lack of maintenance?

For example, this is why you rarely forget information like your childhood address, even if you have not used it for years and years because there are so many connections, and stories, and experiences, around that piece of information.

> Your brain determines critical information and never lets it erode away.

Your brain determines information that is critical and will never let it erode away. Knowing this can benefit us tremendously. The process of SuperLearning necessitates that we create more connections to the information we want to learn. This way the brain is forced to remember the information like it would remember everyday information that we use.

Think about how children learn, for example. They pick up a spoon, and they play with it time and time again. They eat with it; they drop it on the floor; someone picks it up and gives them another one; and the child drops it again. All the while, they are building connections; understanding; a history around that spoon; what the spoon does; and how it feels in their hand and mouth. Finally, they learn to remember the name – spoon.

LEARNING TO CREATE NEW MEMORIES

This is also why writing things down, and/or creating **mnemonics** is a useful tactic for learning. You are simply creating new memories in the form of stories, songs, muscle memories, or sentences. You are associating new information to a word you already know, such as the popular "FOIL" mnemonic in mathematics (first, outer, inner, last for the order of mathematical operations).

As we have said before, we can go far beyond this. We can build connections in a much more efficient and rich way and that is what we are going to be learning.

ASK DR. LEV: NEURONS AND LONG-TERM RETENTION

Neurons are arranged into clusters of neurons that fire together making each other stronger. For long-term retention you do need to connect your new information with an existing strong pattern (prior knowledge), or generate a new strong pattern by collecting many pieces of strongly related information (cool exciting trend) or by spaced repetition (hard work). Weaker relations will help creativity, but will probably not generate long-term retention.

HOMEWORK

Check the Syllabus for homework assignments and recommended supplementary materials.

CHAPTER 8: WHY IMAGES ARE THE MOST POWERFUL WAY TO REMEMBER

CHAPTER OVERVIEW

In this chapter, we do an important exercise to demonstrate how effective your brain is at recognizing a huge amount of information very quickly through imagery.

In the supplementary materials, you will find another *TED* Talk about memory, from a U.S. national memory champion. He started out as a normal guy. He explains how he (and other memory champions) uses vivid imagery to remember long lectures, decks of cards, and so on. We also mention this *TED* Talk in Chapter 27, so you can watch it now or later on in the course.

REMEMBERING PICTURES IS EASIER THAN REMEMBERING WORDS

Evolution has yielded us some pretty interesting skills. We have been telling oral histories for thousands of years. These tales pale in comparison to the amount of time we have been hunting and gathering. For this reason, not only can we spot an approaching predator very quickly, we can also remember pictures far better than spoken words.

This is super useful if you need to remember where you saw that herd of buffalo going, or what that berry looked like that made everyone really, really sick. Because of this evolutionary development, visual information is simply easier to recall than auditory information. It also has to do with the fact that pictures are more encoded.

Pictures are imbued with rich information such as color, context, shape, and size. They are more likely to have a higher number of neural connections (connections between neurons, which send information via neurotransmitters).

Picture Exercise

To demonstrate this, I want to go through an exercise. Below is a picture. I want you to look at the picture for just two seconds. I want you to try to understand as much detail as you can about it in that short amount of time. Then, cover it up with your hand and do not cheat.

What are the people doing? How are they feeling? What is the context? I bet you, if I asked you to, you could write me at least a thousand words about the composition, where things were laid out, what the meaning and significance of the photo is. A photo is just information, and you have just read and remembered thousands of words worth of information in a matter of seconds. ***This demonstrates how effective it is to see things as pictures and symbols rather than auditory information.***

> Learn to **transform** concepts, ideas and other important information **into pictures**. The best types of pictures are **strange, bizarre** or **emotionally connected to memories.**

For this reason, we have to learn to transform concepts, ideas, and other important information into pictures immediately when we encounter the data. The best types of pictures, by the way, are strange, bizarre or emotionally connected to memories. We will be covering that in a little bit more detail soon.

THE NEUROSCIENTIST'S STORY

For now, I want to tell you a pretty interesting story that actually happened while I was building this course. I was chatting with a neuroscientist from Austria. We were talking about the process of learning, neural networks and, specifically, how it related to languages.

We began to talk about different ways to learn, and she recanted a story to me of when she was in med school, long before she started to understand how the brain functioned. Apparently, one of her first tasks was to memorize all of the bones in the human body, which is a momentous task.

She was telling me that she struggled a great deal in memorizing the bones. This was because she was simply looking at the bones in a diagram - a very undetailed image without any emotional connection. She said she struggled and struggled.

Then, the next assignment she had was to memorize all of the ligaments in a human body. The way that the students in the class learned was much more memorable, though: they had to dissect a cadaver from top to bottom. She told me, "I promise you, I will never forget a single ligament in the human body."

One thing that really caught my attention is how she described it. She told me,

"Those images will never leave my mind."

Now, I think it is important to draw a conclusion from this. It is important to realize that in both situations (the textbook with the bone diagrams and the cadavers) there were images involved. However, the **detailed experiential images** of the cadaver, the very concrete minute details were what allowed her to memorize the ligaments much better than the bones.

This is a really interesting segue, because in the next chapters, we are going to be talking about what types of images are most poignant and most memorable, and also how we can better store images laced with significance and meaning to improve our long-term memory.

HOMEWORK

Check the Syllabus for homework assignments and recommended supplementary materials.

Chapter 9: What Types Of Images Come Naturally To You?

Now, there are different types of images, of course, and different types of images will be more effective for different types of people. Let's do a quick test to determine if you choose the **stereotypical** (catalog) image, a **personal** (favorite) image, a **fictional** (comical) image or a **graphical** (drawing) image.

From there, we know what images you should be imagining and which ones will be most effective for you.

I want you to imagine a coffee cup. You can close your eyes if you want or keep them open, but imagine that coffee cup as vividly as possible. What is the design of the coffee cup? How tall is it? How full?

Congratulations - you just created your first "marker."

What type of image did you choose for your marker?

Is it a stereotypical coffee cup that you might have seen in a catalog? Is the cup one you just made up? Is it a coffee cup that you remember from a previous experience? Do you see the cup as a drawing? Take note of this because this is most likely your ideal style of image.

Of course, if you choose a coffee cup that already has neural links, such as the one your mother used to sip from while she made you breakfast, that is best. It will allow you to link new information about coffee and coffee cups in general to those preexisting, deeply encoded memories.

Sometimes you will get personal images and sometimes not. You have to learn to go with what comes naturally, i.e., what pops in your head at the moment. Try to lean towards whatever type of image you find is most conducive for you to remember. Just relax and go with the image that comes to mind.

There are two important points to remember when you start creating these images. First, make sure that the images are as detailed as possible. Not just a coffee cup, but a ruby red coffee cup about half full with a little handle and a textured finish.

Second, make sure that you create connections, memories and stories based on that image, even if it is a fictional one. Imagine a character you know drinking from it. This is very slow going at first. Believe me, I understand that; however, we are working towards building up a **vocabulary of pictures and reference points**, just like you have a vocabulary of words.

Eventually, you should have a mental image (A.K.A. "Marker") for just about everything you wish to remember.

This will give you reference points, and various memories and ideas that you can connect around coffee cups, cars, groups of people, whatever it is.

DR. LEV EXPLAINS IMAGES

You can use any image as long as you infuse it with meaning. This meaning may come from your own life, some fictional or nonfictional histories you know, your creativity, etc. You may combine some or all of the meanings.

Typically, images are either highly creative or highly logical. Imagine you run a Google image search. If your marker is easily recognizable, the initial marker visualization is good enough. The details and links are added to the marker by connecting markers with other information within the text or context.

WHAT IF YOU HAVE A HARD TIME VISUALIZING?

This difficulty is fairly common. Perhaps 10% of people have difficulty visualizing.

Here are our recommendations:

Work to develop this skill. You can view images and then close your eyes and try to recall them. During the recall process, engage as many senses as possible, i.e., how does it feel, smell, taste? It is possible to succeed in this course without developing a strong visual memory, but it will be much more difficult.

Try to see what types of images are easier for you to visualize and focus on them, i.e., comic characters, photographic images, pencil sketches, paintings.

You may have an easier time remembering other sensory information, such as feeling heat or cold, smelling chocolate, etc. If so, that is fine. These sensations can also be markers.

Some students who have difficulty visualizing images find it easier to relate to diagrams or colors as memory points or triggers.

The main point is not to give up. You will figure out something that works for you.

HOMEWORK

Check the Syllabus for homework assignments and recommended supplementary materials.

CHAPTER 10: THE THEORY IN ACTION: LEARNING SOMETHING NEW

This entire chapter is an exercise to practice the use of visual markers, and demonstrate how effective they are.

Let's dive into an exercise. I am going to throw some random concepts at you, and I want you to try to make "markers," or mental images, for each of those concepts:

CALIFORNIA

For example, if an article talks about California, you convert California to an image. I want you to take note of what type of image you chose for California. Is the image stereotypical, personal, fictional or graphical? Try to connect the image of California to one or two existing memories that you have.

WORLD WAR II

Try converting World War II to an image. Is the image a movie you saw with a friend, or a museum you visited? Do not create just a generic concept of World War II such as a warplane; be very specific in creating the image. Can you hear the planes and the bombs? Can you see the flag being raised at Iwo Jima? What is the first image that comes to mind when think of World War II?

NOW, TRY IT ON YOUR OWN

I want you to open any random *Wikipedia* article or use the featured Wiki of the day in your chosen language. I want you to choose about 10 to 20 concepts or ideas in that article, and convert them to images – or what we call "markers".

Once you have those 10 to 20 markers, and you have taken time to link them to your own memories, I want you to try to play them back. Can you name all 10 to 20? Is there a difference between the ones that you do remember and the ones that you do not?

Most likely, the ones you are going to remember are the ones you have best described with highly meaningful and concrete images, images that are well linked to other memories of yours. You can try this a few times and see how you improve over time. If you want a real challenge, I want you to try to remember them in chronological order.

Now, as you go about the rest of your day or week, **try this with anything you are trying to learn**, either for work or school or even in this course. Choose something you want to remember, and create a visual mental marker for it. Get as detailed as possible and see how it actually helps you learn more effectively.

HOMEWORK

Check the Syllabus for homework assignments and recommended supplementary materials.

SECTION 3: USING MENTAL MARKERS FOR LEARNING

CHAPTER 11: WHAT DO PICTURES HAVE TO DO WITH READING?

CHAPTER OVERVIEW

This chapter will help you understand the flow of information from your working memory to your short-term memory and then to your long-term memory. Since most of the learning you do comes through reading (whether speed reading or otherwise), it's important to immediately make the connection between markers and reading We haven't gotten to speed reading yet, but by teaching you how to apply the marker technique to your everyday reading, we ensure that you are well-practiced by the time we *do* get there.

CONVERTING CONCEPTS TO IMAGES

As you probably saw in the *Wikipedia* exercise, converting concepts or other units of knowledge into images makes them much more memorable. For this reason, any concept we wish to remember can and should be converted to a marker.

HOW TO DO THIS WHILE READING

One thing you will notice when we get to speed reading is that you are going to have to take regular pauses. This is not only because it mentally very taxing, but also because we are optimizing the process.

It is kind of like the division of labor in capitalism, or if you have read Tim Ferris' work, "batching like tasks." This is a well-known productivity and efficiency trick. We are just applying it to reading. Let us explain:

THREE STAGES OF MEMORY

There are three stages of memory:

Encoding – adding meaning to the information by converting it into something we understand: acoustic, semantic (meaning), or visual information.

Storage – transferring the encoded information from working memory to short term memory and (hopefully) to long term memory

Retrieval –accessing the newly-stored information, thereby solidifying its neural connections and integrity

Instead of trying to perform all three stages for each and every sentence, we are going to learn how to break these processes into batches and separating them.

MICRO-PAUSES

In applying the marker technique to reading, we take very short micro-pauses after each paragraph or page to move things from our working memory to our short-term memory. Because our working memory lasts about 30 seconds and can hold between 5 and 9 items of information, it is very important that we encode information within that timeframe. For this reason, micro-pauses are a great way to utilize the time that it takes to turn pages.

LONGER PAUSES

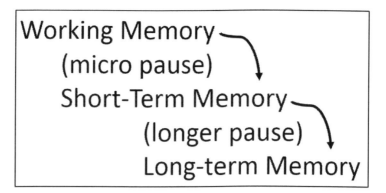

About every 10 minutes, we pause to move information to long-term memory. Ten minutes is about the limit of your short-term memory, so do not neglect this step.

If you do not move this information from short-term memory into long-term memory habitually within every 10 minutes, the information is lost. Remember our hose and bucket metaphor - the funnel can only hold so much, and if you are not transferring information into your long-term memory, you are plugging the bottom of the funnel.

So What Do We Do During Those Pauses?

We take all of our **markers**, the mental images that we've created throughout the text, and

we **record** them,

we **retrieve** them,

we **play them back** in our minds

at the end of each page or each chapter.

Not All Markers Have To Be Images

Now it is worth noting, not all markers have to be visual. In fact, smell is actually a more memorable sense than vision. Of course, we cannot smell an entire book, and so we are focusing on images. If you read about chocolate and you can conjure up the smell or the taste of chocolate that is a great marker.

Whatever type of markers we use, the markers will almost certainly be a mix in the end. **The markers remind us of the details that we have decided we need to remember.** They allow us to move that information from short-term memory to long-term memory very quickly and effectively.

Instead of reading back over the chapter, we think of those 10 or 15 images that we created. We play them back almost like a filmstrip, and that helps our retrieval.

The markers also, as an added benefit, serve as landmarks on the page. Which, if we need extraordinarily detailed information like, "What month was it in 1967?" we can go back, and because we have that landmark (the marker on the page) we know exactly where to find the information.

Eventually, we are going to be teaching you how to sight-read (reading without subvocalization). You will not actually read the individual words. You will be teaching your brain to understand chunks of symbols in large impressions. We will then be training the brain to convert automatically these symbols into written words, or memorable graphical images.

Eventually, you will be able to move your eyes over the text and see a series of images. Which, soon enough, you will learn to store. This is much further down the line, but don't worry, we are getting there.

HOMEWORK

Check the Syllabus for homework assignments and recommended supplementary materials.

CHAPTER 12: CREATING EFFECTIVE MARKERS FOR BETTER MEMORY

CHAPTER OVERVIEW

In this chapter, we go into great detail about the qualities of good markers, as well as how to create them. This is a **very important chapter** for your success, so please pay close attention!

MARKERS

Markers are such a critical aspect of speed learning and SuperLearning that it is worth going back over them. I want to describe what makes a good marker. There are many different elements:

MARKERS ARE HIGHLY SPECIFIC CONCEPTS

A good marker represents a concept, which can be summarized in only one or two words, which is highly, highly detailed and specific.

For example, you would not summarize an entire paragraph as "spaceship" or "moon landing." You would think about the specific detail of the paragraph, for example Neil Armstrong or Buzz Aldrin, and encode that information for a single marker.

MARKERS HAVE HIGHLY DETAILED IMAGERY

The more detailed and specific the marker is the better. Ideally, you want to remember at least four related items or details from each marker.

To give an example, we do not just think of a car. We think of a red Cadillac, with black leather, and polished wheels. We picture the texture of the leather, the shade of the red, how the sun hits it. We do all this in as much detail as we possibly can.

You Can Easily Draw Connections Between Markers

Another important factor is that it is easy to draw the connection between one marker and the next.

For example, the marker Neil Armstrong should automatically remind you of Houston, Apollo 11, the American flag and/or "One small step for man," assuming those were some of your other markers.

You see, by using these highly detailed markers, we are able to remember more details with fewer memory points. We create stronger linkages, or neural networks, between each one of our memory points.

It is a great cheat, because if we go from the details back to the original concept that works great. However, if I tell you the original concept, for example moon landing, you might forget the details. **We focus on memorizing those details, and we can reverse engineer the overall concept, meaning, and context from them.**

Markers Are Easily And Quickly Converted Into Images

Another great aspect of a good marker is that you are able to convert it easily and quickly into an image (or a feeling or smell).

For example, I can quickly convert DNA, into an image of a double helix; however, I personally cannot create an image for genetics. That is a hard concept to visualize, and so I go with the double helix.

Remember The Solution Or Resolution

Another important thing to remember, if the paragraph you are reading presents a problem and a solution, or a conflict and a resolution, it is always better to remember the solution or resolution, never the question. If you have the solution, for example, a broken up Germany, you can remember where the conflict or the problem came from, in this case, World War II.

GENERAL GUIDELINES FOR MARKERS

You should try to create a marker for every single important detail. For example, people, dates, formulas, events, but this is not all.

You should have 2 to 4 markers per paragraph depending on the density of the material and the length of the paragraph.

This works out to be about 10 to 20 markers per page. Now you will not always create that many, and you certainly will not always remember that many, but that is fine. It is better to be mindful and create all of these markers for significant details you wish to remember. This way, if you forget one of your markers, you can reverse engineer as we have mentioned before.

Again, we will be able to reverse engineer and remember other markers if we have sufficiently detailed and connected markers. It is going to take time, and you are going to have to practice to create high quality markers quickly. You will know your markers are improving when you are able to summarize and deduct the entire meaning of a concept or story simply by recalling the long list of markers you have.

REVIEW OF WHAT MAKES A HIGH QUALITY MARKER

That was quite a bit to take in. Here is a review of what we have learned about high quality markers.

1. High quality markers represent details that can be **described in 1 to 2 words**, not overall concepts.

2. High quality markers are themselves **encoded with rich detail**, such as colors, textures and so on.

3. High quality markers are **interconnected clearly and logically** to one another both backwards and forwards.

4. High quality markers **emphasize outcomes or resolutions** not questions or initial conflicts.

5. High quality markers **come in great numbers**. The more, the merrier.

Now, choosing good and detailed markers will allow you this reverse engineering. We are using the bottom-up method instead of the top-down. It is easier to remember these details and then deduct how we arrived.

EXERCISE

In the Syllabus for this chapter, you are going to find a game or exercise that I want you to try. The game will give you a few images, and then swarm them in a bunch of other images, and you are supposed to remember which ones were the remembered images.

Try this doing it without markers or detail, and then try encoding each one of these images. If there is an image of a rabbit, think of a childhood friend who had a rabbit, and picture playing with that rabbit. Try again and see how much more effective you are when you carefully encode details.

Play with this for 10 minutes a day until you see a dramatic improvement. It will really help when we get to speed reading.

ASK DR. LEV:
HOW LONG DOES IT TAKE TO GENERATE A MARKER? – PART 1

One of the most interesting questions starring in the latest discussions is "How long does it take to generate a visual marker?" When we describe generation of visual markers, we include several different activities that light up different parts of the brain. Some of them take longer; others are lightning fast. Moreover, the complexity of the task is inversely proportional to the amount of experience in the particular area. I will try to address different sides of the issue.

What are the activities involved in creating a visual marker?

When we create visual markers, we perform at least some of the activities below:

- Analyze the concept of interest and its attributes
- Generate visual associations
- Assign an object/icon to represent the concept
- Define several details associated with specific context in which the concept appears and encode them as colors or shapes of the object elements
- Analyze connections of the concept with other concepts within the context and within the whole body of knowledge
- Encode the connection links as physical placement or motion and indicate an element generating the link
- Verify that we encoded only the details that are relevant and encode all the details that are relevant...

There may be other activities involved, or we may have missed some activities that are specific to a particular method or field of knowledge.

How complex is a marker?

Clearly, it is hard to do all the tasks involved with sufficient accuracy. *An average visual marker I use has 3-4 details encoded into it and has 3-4 connections to other markers.* Moreover, it may have color and size, fade-in and fade-out animation corresponding to its context. Therefore, it is about 10 pieces of information per marker.

How do I generate markers fast?

Fortunately, we are usually reading documents that appear very similar to each other. This means that about 90% of what a skilled reader reads has already generated some markers in his/her brain. ***Probably about 70% of the marker details may be reused.*** This means that if we focus only on the new stuff, we have to encode from scratch much less than half of what we read. As long as we do not modify the markers – and we do our best NOT TO MODIFY the markers, we could work pretty fast. It is much easier to add a feature or attribute to an existing template than generate a new template.

Generating brand new markers

When generating brand new markers, it is very important to **understand the whole context of the marker** before we generate the marker, otherwise we would need to modify the marker. Here pre-reading kicks in. If you find something brand-new when pre-reading a paragraph/section, you should stop and generate the marker. You need to make sure that the marker is sufficiently wide and accurate so that you will not change it later on. Typically, the generic marker would be icon-like representation or stylized object. You fill in the missing details as you reread the paragraph or deepen your knowledge in the subject.

How many markers do I use per text?

The density of information within text may vary wildly. Some texts are not very informative, and your reading speed will be limited by your saccade speed (~3000 wpm). In this case, you will probably have a marker per section. Some will include 2-3 markers per sentence and your reading speed will drop to ~200 wpm. However, on average you will end up with a marker per paragraph and reading speed of ~1000 wpm.

PROF. ANNA EXPLAINS MARKERS TO A STUDENT

KL: Hi Anna, would you be able to give me a few examples of very specific questions? Just want to make sure the questions I am asking myself are specific enough.

Anna: "WH" (who, what, when, where, why, how) Questions that can be asked in every article are generic, but if you combine them with a word or marker from the text you have a specific question. Send me an article or a paragraph with markers from pre-reading and some questions that you can ask and assume on them.... Is it helpful?

KL: So I think I understand markers better. Every person reading an article may have a different set of markers depending on which words/images help them remember the most details. Is this correct?

Anna: Yes. But they should be around the same specific important idea...

KL: Okay. For example the following paragraph: Napoléon Bonaparte, born Napoleone di Buonaparte; 15 August 1769 – 5 May 1821, was a French military and political leader who rose to prominence during the latter stages of the French Revolution and its associated wars. As Napoleon I, he was Emperor of the French from 1804 to 1814 and again in 1815.

Marker: French Revolution

Questions:

- **What** strategy did Napoleon use to lead the French through the French Revolution?

- **Where** did the start of the French revolution take place?

- **Which** city?

- **Which** date did the French revolution start?

- **When** did it end?
- **How** did Napoleon become the leader of the French Revolution?

Marker: French Revolution—> reminds me of an image of when I was walking near the Arc de Triumph in Paris, and I imagine a crowd of people protesting and fighting 20 feet from the monument.

Anna: See that in two of the questions the answer is name and number so you can find that info from scanning. You need an article to raise specific questions because your knowledge might not be enough...

KL: Okay, so the questions I would need to raise would need answers that include the entire concepts in the paragraph?

Anna: Yes!

KL: Got it, and if they do not, then I should not be using the word as a marker. Would you be able to give me a good, specific question based on the paragraph I just sent you?

Anna: The **marker** of this paragraph.: **political leader**

1. **What** kind of a leader? French military and political leader

2. **How** he became a leader and when? Rose to prominence during the latter stages of the French Revolution and its associated wars.

3. **What** was the picture of his leadership? He was Emperor of the French from 1804 to 1814 and again in 1815.

This is one way....

This was after reading...

KL: Okay this makes a lot of sense.

So in general, marker—> the word that allows you to remember the highest amount of details in a paragraph

> **Specific questions on the marker—> help you remember the specific details and provide questions that can potentially be answered later in the article.**
> And at the end of each paragraph, I visualize the chosen marker as specific, and detailed as possible.

ASK DR. LEV: CREATIVITY 101: THE POWER OF MULTIPLE PERSPECTIVES

Making great markers requires a lot of creative thinking, and you may struggle at the beginning. Fortunately, it has been proven that creativity is something we learn, not something we are born with. Here is some great advice from Dr. Lev and Prof. Anna on how to become a better creative thinker:

While I had a long and organized training on creativity, Anna is a master of out-of-the-box thinking. She claims that she uses one, and only one trick, but she perfected using it. Anna calls this trick **"multiple perspectives."**

Draw down a shape or write a word. Now take two minutes and write as many associations as you can. Average number is 15. I can do 40 on a good day, limited more by writing speed than by creative potential. How do I come up with 40 uses for a finger or 40 objects that look like a rectangle in two minutes alone? I am utilizing the power of perspectives.

I have an array of perspectives I always try:
- What is this item made of?
- How can I use this item?
- What every day object looks like this item?
- How this item can be used for ... (war, food, construction, art, entertainment, sports, grooming)
- What historic or symbolic meaning is associated with this item?
- Where I can see similar items in the nature?

I have many more of these questions, and I ask them very fast. Each question projects the item into a range of virtual landscapes where I try to fit the item. For each landscape, I get several perfect fits for the item, or a reason for failure, and thus, a link to the next landscape to try.

A similar task of multiple perspectives is given by medium-level visualization: we take an item and rotate it (a topological operation will do) in a 3D space. With each new angle of the marker, we get new details and colors, each detail and color associated with details and colors of the knowledge we are trying to encode.

A third task of perspectives opens up the hyperlinking process. When viewing a new piece of data we try to project it on various bodies of knowledge we already have in our heads, and if there is a connection, we generate a link between the marker and the existing object.

Try out these exercises yourself.

HOMEWORK

Check the Syllabus for homework assignments and recommended supplementary materials.

CHAPTER 13: DEMONSTRATION: CREATING MARKERS AS WE READ

CHAPTER OVERVIEW

In this Chapter, we will be reading a *Wikipedia* article on the Garden City Movement, and describing markers as we go along. This will help you understand which words are marker-worthy (and why), as well as the level of detail expected for each marker.

MARKER CREATION

So let's go ahead and see an example of what marker creation looks like. I am going to go through a portion of a *Wikipedia* article on the Garden City Movement. As I go through the paragraphs, I will describe the kind of markers that I am picking out and try to describe them in vivid detail. Then I will be mapping them and I will try to find images that somewhat come close to the markers that come to mind for me.

This is going to allow you to understand exactly what I mean when I say detailed vivid imagery and to understand which type of words I am creating markers.

Here is the link to the article, for your reference: http://jle.vi/gcm.

In order to demonstrate how I make markers, each paragraph is quoted below, with a table below the paragraph describing each marker.

PARAGRAPH 1

"The garden city movement is a method of urban planning that was initiated in 1898 by Sir Ebenezer Howard in the United Kingdom. Garden cities were intended to be planned, self-contained communities surrounded by "greenbelts," containing proportionate areas of residences, industry and agriculture."

ARTICLE	MARKER CREATION
The garden city movement 	The first thing I noticed, obviously, is **Garden City Movement**. Now, I happen to live in a garden city of Tel Aviv, and so I picture Rothschild Boulevard, which is a very green area. I am picturing a specific block in front of a specific restaurant that I know where the trees are particularly vivid, green, and full of life.
The garden city movement is a method of urban planning that was initiated in **1898...**	The next thing I notice is 1898. It is tough for me to find a marker for that, so I do not particularly come up with one.
...by Sir Ebenezer Howard 	The next thing I am going to notice is Ebenezer Howard. Now, Ebenezer is a pretty rare name. I only have one neural node for that name and it is Ebenezer Scrooge, so I come up with him.

...in the United Kingdom.	United Kingdom - I actually do not come up with the flag of the United Kingdom because sometimes for me it is confusing with the other commonwealth flags. Instead, I actually come up with a map of England, specifically, but kind of the entire United Kingdom.
Garden cities were intended to be planned, self-contained communities surrounded by "**greenbelts**," containing proportionate areas of residences, industry and agriculture.	Garden Cities, Greenbelts – that is pretty easy, I come up with a green leather belt. Particularly I see it on a pair of blue jeans, but a green belt in general.

MOVING ON TO THE NEXT PARAGRAPH IN THE ARTICLE

"Inspired by the Utopian novel *Looking Backward* and Henry George's work *Progress and Poverty,* Howard published his book *To-morrow: a Peaceful Path to Real*

Reform in 1898 (which was reissued in 1902 as *Garden Cities of To-morrow*). His idealised garden city would house 32,000 people on a site of 6,000 acres (2,400 ha), planned on a concentric pattern with open spaces, public parks and six radial boulevards, 120 ft (37 m) wide, extending from the centre. The garden city would be self-sufficient and when it reached full population, another garden city would be developed nearby. Howard envisaged a cluster of several garden cities as satellites of a central city of 50,000 people, linked by road and rail."

Inspired by the **Utopian** novel...	I see the word Utopian and in that, I see a white marble city square with strings of water running up to a fountain. I see this in very vivid detail.
...Looking Backward	I do not have anything for looking backward immediately, but I picture a guy in a top hat, looking over his shoulder.
...and Henry George's...	Now Henry George, those both happen to be names of British kings. Therefore, I imagine an image of King George during the King's Speech, the father, not the son.

...work Progress and **Poverty...**	Progress and Poverty, for the word poverty, I actually I see children during the Great Depression standing in line.
... Howard published his book *To-morrow: a Peaceful Path to Real Reform* in 1898 (which was reissued in **1902** as *Garden Cities* of *To-morrow*).	Garden Cities of Tomorrow, I already have a marker for the Garden City. I happen to know that in 1902 there was a World Fair scheduled to be held in New York but was cancelled. I am envisioning a cancelled World Fair. I am envisioning people reeling back machinery back into a warehouse.

His idealized garden city would house **32,000...**	For 32,000, that is kind of a strange number. The first thing that comes to mind for me is that is exactly 32 gigabytes, which is roughly 32,000 megabytes? Therefore, I actually picture an iPhone because that is a product that comes in a variant of 32 gigabytes.
...people on a site of **6,000** acres...	6,000 - Nothing particularly comes to mind very quickly. However, it is acres so I might picture a huge field of land.
... (2,400 ha), planned on a concentric pattern with open spaces, public parks and six **radial...**	Six **radial** boulevards - for that, I actually picture a hub and spoke, kind of like a wagon wheel. Radial is the word I want there.
... **boulevards**, 120 ft (37 m) wide, extending from the centre.	Boulevards - I picture a planned community where I bought my first house, which is called **Boulevard**.

| Howard envisaged a cluster of several garden cities as **satellites** of a central city of 50,000 people, linked by road and rail.  | We have a cluster of several Garden Cities as **satellites**. For this I actually just picture probably what is in reality, a space telescope - the Hubble space telescope. It is probably kind of a strange example, but I have a very vivid image of what that satellite looks like. That is easy for me to come up with and just jump to it right away. |

THE NEXT PARAGRAPH:

"Howard's *To-morrow: A Peaceful Path to Real Reform* sold enough copies to result in a second edition, *Garden Cities of To-morrow*. This success provided him the support necessary to pursue the chance to bring his vision into reality. Howard believed that all people agreed the overcrowding and deterioration of cities was one of the troubling issues of their time. He quotes a number of respected thinkers and their disdain of cities. Howard's garden city concept combined the town and country in order to provide the working class an alternative to working on farms or 'crowded, unhealthy cities'."

Howard's To-morrow: A Peaceful Path to Real Reform	**Peaceful Path to Real Reform** - For this, I actually picture an Israeli and Palestinian flag. It is kind of my personal marker for reform and peace.
... sold enough copies to result in a second edition, **Garden Cities** of To-morrow.	**Garden Cities** – Again, that same marker jumps back to my mind of Rothschild Boulevard.
This success provided him the support necessary to pursue the chance to bring his vision into reality. Howard believed that all people agreed the **overcrowding and deterioration** of cities was one of the troubling issues of their time.	Here, I immediately jumped to the phrase **overcrowding and deterioration**. **Overcrowding** - I actually see a huge square of people pushing and shoving, just complete chaos.

| He quotes a number of respected thinkers and their disdain of cities. Howard's garden city concept combined the town and country in order to provide the **working class** an alternative to working on farms or 'crowded, unhealthy cities'.

 | Working class, the first thing that comes to me here, is actually someone in very dirty overalls. One of the straps of the overall is left loose. It is as if the overalls are hanging off his body. I can literally see the dirt under his fingernails. Maybe he is a coal miner. I can see his particular hairstyle. It is like someone out of the movie *O Brother, Where Art Thou*. Again, I can see a very detailed, vivid image here. |

This should give you an idea of the words that I am choosing, and you will notice that sometimes I will just skip over particular words or concepts, like 6000. I could not come up with something very quick for that and so I chose to make a marker for 32,000 instead. You also notice that I took very particular details, not kind of the overall pictures, but specific details.

I have Henry George now in my memory. I have 32,000 in my memory. I have overcrowding in my memory. Because I just need to play back these detailed images. What that is going to give me is an overall picture of what was happening during the time that the Garden City Movement was promoted.

I now can deduce from the details that it was a response to overcrowding. It was a response to criticism from the working classes that cities were becoming too crowded. I also know, from my marker of 1902 and my marker of Ebenezer, **who** was doing the promoting and **who** was really bringing this movement to life and **where** he was.

I encourage you to play around with this, keep trying it, and keep practicing it. I hope that this chapter has helped you see the concrete, in-practice way of creating markers.

HOMEWORK

Check the Syllabus for homework assignments and recommended supplementary materials.

CHAPTER 14: LINKING MARKERS

CHAPTER OVERVIEW

We will cover how to link markers together for optimal retention.

LINKING MARKERS FOR LONG-TERM STORAGE

Now that you understand the basics of creating markers, it is important to learn specifically how you should work with them. We have received many requests for clarification and further explanation regarding linking markers. This chapter will cover some of the more difficult areas that students typically struggle with in this area. It can be especially difficult to retain a high percentage of markers after you have been reading for an extended period of time. This chapter will help us in understanding how to link markers for longer-term storage.

MARKER GROUPS

As we mentioned earlier, **markers usually come in groups**. They can be grouped by **similarity** (or what is known as the "tree" data structure) or directly connected with each other in what has called the "**linked list**" data structure. There are also more complex structures to group markers for advanced students, but we will not discuss them right now.

What is important to know is that **you need some way to link your markers together effectively**. By doing this, you create more dense networks of the points, memories, or images, and you are much more likely to remember them.

EXAMPLE - 20-ITEM GROCERY LIST

Let's illustrate this with an example. Suppose you need to go to the local store and buy 20 items. By now, you know well enough to you need to create 20 markers - one for each of these important items. However, how do you link those items together to ensure that none of them is a single, unconnected memory that drifts off into the sea of your mind?

Later on in the course, when we talk about memory palaces, we are going to explain how you can connect all of the memories very quickly and effectively to a physical space or location - but for now, let's think about the several other potent strategies for remembering the 20 markers or items on your grocery list.

In one example, you can divide or "**chunk**" the list into departments: milk products (milk, cheese and yoghurt), meat products (three sorts of sausage, chicken breast, and steak) and so on. You could try to visualize the packages you get at each department. Since each package is below 7 items (this is a "must" for this method), you will be able to recall the visual image per department with great detail. As we mentioned, this is a LOT like a memory palace, but you do not have to worry about all that just yet.

In another example, you could **build a story** and visualize a sort of animation of your mother milking a cow and preparing cheese from the milk, then throwing in some jam to make yoghurt instead, since your niece has a sweet tooth. Imagine that your niece is missing 3 teeth, and that makes it difficult for her to bite off a chunk of sausage. Then, the niece laughs, calls your mother a chicken breast, runs away, and falls. At the end of the story, your mother puts a frozen steak on the bump on her head.

This is a ridiculous story - but it is so ridiculous that you are not likely to forget it any time soon.

CONNECTING THE MARKERS FROM CHAPTER 13 - GARDEN CITIES

If we apply this to the markers from the last chapter on demonstrating marker creation, we might get something like Ebenezer Scrooge and King Henry the 8th riding in an overcrowded carriage with Radial Wheels through King George's green flower garden on their way to the 1902 World's

Fair. That one image contains 7 markers from the last chapter all strung together in an easy-to-remember story. All we have to remember is this one "package" of markers, and we remember 7 very specific details about the Garden City Movement.

By "linking" these markers in a quick and dirty way into a vividly memorable story or a set of "chunked" images in the first example, you have been able to recall many more markers than you would if you had just made a simple list.

Eventually, you should be able to combine both methods – chunking and building a story. You should not have lists of more than 20 objects (preferably limited to 7-9) and should not have chunks of more than 7 objects each (preferably limited to 3-4). You can then cut open each object and see another list or package within.

TEXT ORGANIZATION

Each text we read is organized in a similar structure by the internal logic of text:
- The text is divided into sections.
- A section is divided into paragraphs.
- A paragraph is divided into sentences.

Never try to memorize a marker outside of its context - the markers should be remembered within a package or a story, interconnected to other markers in that specific area.

This is a bit overwhelming, I know, but bear with me.

When you try to remember a list, you should visualize the first and the last item in the list in more detail than the other markers. Then, you will be able to recreate the story both from the beginning and from the end.

It is a good idea to practice creating the story from both the beginning and the end. Do not spend much time imagining the middle markers, as long as you have a unique mental animation to connect these markers to the before and after markers.

When you visualize a package marker, the whole package appears as a marker with each item within the package as a detail of the marker.

This visualization is great for the markers that represent physical objects, but does not really work for abstract notions. ***For abstract notions, you can visualize icons***. For example, war is two swords, a contract is handshake, peace is an olive branch, etc. Do you remember the example I gave of making a marker for genetics versus DNA and the double helix? These abstract notions can be connected by some kind of logical arrow that indicates cause, contradiction, and/or conclusion.

When making packaged markers, try to avoid inserting information that was not originally in the text, because you will likely remember that information also. Therefore, it probably is not a great idea to add the "carriage" to my example above unless I am sure I will not forget that the radial wheels are what matter.

We really want to make the recall process as simple and non-ambiguous as possible. It is important that you experiment with the different ways of chunking and packaging markers, and different levels of ridiculous markers to determine what a good fit is for you. These tricks of linking and chunking markers will make huge improvements to your ability to retain the markers long-term.

However, for material that you need to memorize with near 100% efficiency, you can refer to the advanced chapter on memory palaces, towards the end of the course.

HOMEWORK

Check the Syllabus for homework assignments and recommended supplementary materials.

CHAPTER 15: TRYING OUT YOUR NEW SKILLS

CHAPTER OVERVIEW

In this chapter, we give you guidance for trying out your new skills in everyday life, which you should consider as important homework!

USE YOUR SKILLS

As we are going to talk about a little bit later, your success really depends on you using your skills and finding that they are useful in your daily life. *If you do not think these skills are useful, you will not put in the effort, the skill will never be developed and the goal of becoming a SuperLearner is not going to happen.*

Your homework is to try these new skills out with anything and everything in your daily life. Later on, we will be teaching you great techniques to apply the method to other things, but for now, get creative and see how you can adapt it yourself.

For example, the next time a friend tells you a story, or you walk into the other room to grab something, try creating some markers. This is a cool way to avoid walking into the kitchen and forgetting what you came in there to retrieve. Another cool thing is that when you meet people, you can use this trick, but we will be covering that in due time.

Create a marker before you pick up the phone if you are in the middle of doing something. It will be extremely easy to remember what you were doing and go back to your workflow if you have that detailed marker.

Eventually, I want you to create an automatic habit or a reflex, that anytime you are distracted or anytime you are embarking on a new task you are creating a marker.

You would not close a book without reflexively putting in a bookmark, would you? This is the same principle. I want you to create markers as bookmarks to remind you what you were doing. The more you do this, the faster and more natural it is going to become, and that is going to make a huge difference in your ability and ease in creating markers.

You may not be speed reading yet, but if you can get really, really effective at creating high quality markers, it is going to be much faster and much easier to improve your retention when we do get to the speed reading portion of the course.

Do that homework, and make sure that you are learning how to create high quality markers.

HOMEWORK

Check the Syllabus for homework assignments and recommended supplementary materials.

SECTION 4: PRE-READING AND PREPARATION

CHAPTER 16: PRE-READ BEFORE YOU READ

CHAPTER OVERVIEW:

In this chapter, we are going to learn a bit about pre-reading.

PRE-READING THE TEXT

Great news! We have only one more section until we get to the sexy stuff. For now though, we are going to talk about pre--reading.

Now, pre-reading may seem counterintuitive, since speed is our goal here, but **for any text where the goal is to remember detail and structure, we strongly recommend pre-reading** the text. This is especially important for dense materials or mixed reading with lots of pictures, such as textbooks.

Now, I probably would not pre-read a novel for fear of spoiling the plot, but if I do, I will look for areas of conversations and dialogue and determine the outline and flow of the chapter.

When we pre-read a text, we are taking a **few seconds per page** at a speed about **5 to 8 times your current speed**. We are just **looking for titles, sub-headings, proper nouns, numbers, words**, or things that just do not seem to fit in. When we pre-read, we **gain an understanding of the structure of the text** and we **build** a sort of **mental map**.

We think, "Oh, this is interesting. They are going to talk about Buzz Aldrin here," for example. These will serve as **temporary markers** and we will be able to **replace them later with much more detailed, high-quality markers** when we actually read the text. The Pareto principle, or 80/20 rule that we talked about, which Tim Ferris loves so much, is very helpful here.

We are looking for 20% of the details that give us an 80% understanding of what we are going to be reading or at least what the text is about. In the long term, once you become skilled enough at creating markers, you will be able to spot and store high quality markers even in your pre-reading.

This means that when you actually read the text, all you have to do is fill in those two to four details we talked about for each marker and you are well on your way. This will take a lot of time, but it is a pivotal skill in speed reading and it will differentiate skimming from actually learning the content you are reading at a high level.

It is important to note that even though you do not register the text, you are building a map of it and becoming more familiar with it subconsciously, as if you begin to understand the layout of a neighborhood even if you drive through it at 40 miles an hour. Do not get frustrated and do not let yourself become hung up on understanding the text. Just **build a very rudimentary map or understanding of the structure**.

HOMEWORK

Check the Syllabus for homework assignments and recommended supplementary materials.

CHAPTER 17: CREATING AN INTENSE INTEREST AND CURIOSITY

CHAPTER OVERVIEW

In this chapter, we are going to examine the work of Malcolm Knowles, the foremost authority on adult learning, to understand some of the requirements for adults to obtain new knowledge. Integrating these elements is going to be an integral part of our pre-reading strategy, as we will see that creating and promoting curiosity and applicability of the knowledge is a crucial success factor.

In this chapter, you are assigned a homework assignment of incorporating interest and curiosity into your daily reading. Please note that while interest and curiosity have a place in all forms of reading, if you are reading extremely dense materials, you may need multiple pre-readings to generate this interest and curiosity (to be covered later). At the very least, please remember to pre-read and practice using your lighter readings of the day, such as newspapers, pleasure reading, or emails.

MALCOLM KNOWLES AND THE SIX REQUIREMENTS FOR ADULT LEARNING

In the 1950s, one of the leading researchers in adult education, Malcolm Knowles, published a book around the six requirements for adult learning. Most important among these rules, Knowles described that adult learners are unique in that they require not only a learning environment that harnesses their previous experiences, but also the appropriate readiness, a pressing need, and an immediate application of the knowledge they wish to acquire.

For example, whereas children are able to learn multiplication tables just because mom said so, adults are generally unable to learn unless they can see a pressing and relevant need, and use for that information. This explains why a lot of us fail at learning new skills or languages. We may have the desire, but we do not have the immediate application.

To get around this, you should use your pre-reading time to inspire within yourself a burning curiosity or interest in what the text is about, and you should think about how you should apply it. Now, even the most uninteresting material, such as law, can benefit from this practice.

As you read throughout the text, try to envision scenarios in which they could affect your life, or how you could benefit from having that knowledge. Of course, as we mentioned before, try to connect any markers you develop to existing knowledge or experiences in your long-term memory. Beyond this, you are going to see a huge improvement in reading and comprehension if you develop questions and curiosities within the text.

Perhaps they mention Baltimore, Maryland. Ask yourself, "What the heck does Baltimore have to do with real estate law? What happened there? Was there a precedent set?" Find things that do not seem to fit in, and ask yourself what they are doing there.

Dr. Lev once gave me some great questions to raise because I was struggling with pre-reading myself.

He told me to think about how I can use this material in my day-to-day life, where the author might be wrong, where I may disagree with the ideas, how this material could be improved, or what I would expect to see in the text that I am not seeing at this speed.

When you return to the normal speed of reading and you go back over the chapter, you will have a lot of questions that you are very eager to answer, and this is a huge tool for concentration. If you suffer from attention deficit, you know that if you really want something, you can be laser focused.

If you want to know why the heck Baltimore is in this text, you will come back and you will focus harder than you ever imagined you would focus on real estate law.

HOMEWORK

There is a little bit of homework for this section. I want you to incorporate pre-reading and questions, and curiosity and interests into things that you are normally reading.

If you are a student, this means you pick the most boring text from that Econ class and try pre-reading it. For work, do the same. I want you to work on building that intense curiosity and envisioning that practical use for the information. It does not seem like it would make a big difference, but trust me, it does.

Pre-read any material you read. Practice creating questions & curiosity

Check the Syllabus for homework assignments and recommended supplementary materials.

SECTION 5: READ WITH YOUR EYES, NOT WITH YOUR INNER VOICE

CHAPTER 18: HOW MOST PEOPLE READ: SUBVOCALIZATION

CHAPTER OVERVIEW

"Subvocalization" is the enemy of speed and comprehension. In this chapter, we are going to learn what that means, and why it is true. Then, we are going to begin to understand how speed-readers overcome subvocalization, with an introduction to the mechanics of separated information processing.

SPEED READING

We have finally arrived at the sexiest part of the course, speed-reading. Let's first start by understanding how most people (including you, most likely) read.

SUBVOCALIZATION

When most people read, they actually hear the words in their mental voice. This is a process called **subvocalization**, and they go along the text and *hear* "The quick brown fox jumped over the lazy dog."

This is because when we are taught to read, we have to sound it out. We do not know how words look visually, and so we sound out F-O-X, fox, or we sound out the word phonetically as Fa-Ah-Kxs, fox.

This is a very hard habit to break, because it is how we learned. We associate words not with the meaning or content, but with the sounds.

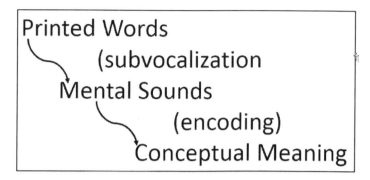

Printed Words
          (subvocalization
Mental Sounds
          (encoding)
Conceptual Meaning

Then, we encode the sounds into conceptual meaning.

As we have learned already, this is hugely inefficient. You are taking high quality visual information and symbols, and you are degrading the quality and bandwidth. The maximum speed that any subvocalizing reader can attain is about 250 words a minute. Most speed readers can at least break 600 or 700, even breaking 1,000 like Lev.

Furthermore, when you lean on subvocalization, you will be much more easily distracted by noise, and you will have lower comprehension and retention.

This is because there are three things happening at once, as we learned before – the encoding, the storage and retrieval.

When you subvocalize, you are trying to condense all three into one moment.

BREAKING THE "SOUND BARRIER"

In speed-reading, however, we learn to read much quicker than the sound barrier. This necessitates that we use a more efficient process for learning. We suppress that inner voice, and we instead start to recognize words as what they are - symbols. We also break apart the three processes of reading.

Now if you have read Tim Ferris *The 4-Hour Workweek*, you are familiar with the concept of batching like tasks, and we have discussed this before. If you studied process operations management, it is a lot like that as well.

First, we are going to encode the information using rapid, efficient eye movements. From there, the mind is trained to quickly and automatically store information into our working memory using emotionally significant markers or reference points.

We have covered that already. Remember?

Finally, we take periodic pauses at the end of pages or chapters as we mentioned before, and we perform retrieval, which conscientiously moves the most detailed information possible into the long-term memory. By breaking this apart into separate steps, we are both more efficient, and more effective.

Let's start trying it out.

ASK DR. LEV: SUBVOCALIZATION SUPPRESSION TRAINING

The brain cannot efficiently perform two vocalizations at the same time. This training not only teaches you speed reading, but also opens you to efficient multitasking.

This exercise is the simplest way to reduce subvocalization when reading text line by line.

Choose to visualize one marker per line. You are allowed to subvocalize 1-2 words per line.

BEGINNER

Slowly (100wpm) repeat aloud as you are reading the words, sentences and paragraphs, 2-4-6-8-10. Your job is to count by multiples of 2s as you read along. After you reach 10, continue reading, but start-over, 2-4-6-8-10, and so forth, to the bottom of the page. Do not focus on the counting; let it become a mindless song, a jingle. Your job is to focus above the words and feel your eyes sweep left – middle – right, sentence-after-sentence.

INTERMEDIATE

Now "silently" do the "2, 4, 6, 8, 10s," while reading. You can mentally raise-the-volume on hearing the numbers, and it will drown-out the subvocalization of the words. Our left-brain is a serial-processor; it can only run one program at a time. When we focus on hearing the numbers it is like a jingle that gets in your mind and will not leave, and that song takes prominence over the subvocalizing the words.

EXPERT

The objective is to not need the numbers, and not hear the words you read. Open up a TV or radio or another noise source and focus in on what you are reading. Make the brain focus on the text a hand and not on the conversation on TV. Now slow down your reading and focus on the conversation. Try to understand the conversation while reducing the reading speed to compensate. Continue for 3 minutes and switch your focus back to the text.

HOMEWORK

Check the Syllabus for homework assignments and recommended supplementary materials.

CHAPTER 19: SACCADES: USING YOUR EYES AS EFFECTIVELY AS POSSIBLE

CHAPTER OVERVIEW

In this chapter, we learn about "saccades," or rapid jumps of the eye. This is a central tenet of speed reading, and so we begin to practice them and train our eyes to perform them effectively.

We then spend some time talking about adapting reading material to fit our preferred number of saccades, and making sure font sizes and text formatting are suitable for fast absorption. We learn to use plugins and apps that improve our reading experience.

Finally, we apply our new skill to a fun game, to see what a difference they make in our ability to recognize new information rapidly.

TWO OR THREE SEPARATE COLUMNS ON THE PAGE

1   **2**   **3**

cret agent in more decisions than we could imagine. It even helps us decide whom to date—and, ultimately, whom to marry. Let me describe an experiment that explored just this subject.

As students hurried around MIT one cold weekday, I asked some of them whether they would allow me to take their pictures for a study. In some cases, I got disapproving looks. A few students walked away. But most of them were happy to participate, and before long, the card in my digital camera was filled with images of smiling students. I returned to my office and printed 60 of them—30 of women and 30 of men.

The following week I made an unusual request of 25 of my undergraduates. I asked them to pair the 30 photographs of men and the 30 of women by physical attractiveness (matching the men with other men, and the women with other women). That is, I had them pair the Brad Pitts and the George Clooneys of MIT, as well as the Woody Allens and the Danny De-Vitos (sorry, Woody and Danny). Out of these 30 pairs, I selected the six pairs—three female pairs

When we speed read, the first thing we do is imagine two or three separate columns on the page, and we train our eyes to jump between them.

> **Saccade** (noun): A rapid movement of the eye between fixation points

Our eyes are not capable of smooth, gradual movements. They actually make very precise and speedy jumps, and **these jumps are called saccades**. When you dart your eyes across the room, because you see something in your peripheral vision, you move very quickly and refocus very quickly. That is a saccade.

Normal readers do 10 to 20 micro saccades on a page - usually one for every word. However, because our eyes are not focused or absorbing information while they are in motion, this number of saccades is hugely inefficient. Speed readers minimize the number of saccades. We use two or three in a normal book like this one, and four to five in a full width webpage. We learn to do this as quickly as possible.

We try to format the text into the appropriate width for two to three saccades if we have an option. We will cover e-readers and browser extensions and things like that later. However, when formatting the text is not possible, we try to think in advance, during our pre-reading, how many saccades are necessary.

For example, in a small printed newspaper column, or an electronic device such as your cell phone, one saccade is usually enough. If we are reading on an iPad, or on our browser, we can probably use something like Instapaper or Pocket or even Safari's built in reading extension. This will allow you to store the articles you want to read in stripped-down formats.

From there, you can set the text size and even the column size to be appropriate for two to three saccades. Anna and I recommend three. Three saccades appear to be the most effective with all the students she has taught. This one trick of jumping in saccades is pretty much the gist of what Tim Ferriss preaches in his *PX Method.*

It is the basis for all speed reading. However, what Tim misses, and why I always failed to speed read when I tried the *PX Method*, is the memory and the optimization of these saccades. So, let's jump in and see how we get past 450 words per minute with 20 to 30% comprehension.

GET ACQUAINTED WITH ALL YOUR DIFFERENT DEVICES

By the way, the homework for this chapter is to acquaint yourself with all your different electronic devices from your Kindle to your iPad to your browser. In addition, if some of your devices do not have a reading mode, sign up for Pocket or Instapaper and learn how to use these devices with columns, and formatted reading in the proper size for your eye span.

I personally love to use Safari's reading mode and I have a keyboard shortcut set for that. However, if you are using an iPad or iPhone there is a handy button on the top left that will allow you to switch right into reading mode. If you are using the Google Chrome or Mozilla Firefox browsers, you are going to need to download an extension, from either the Google Chrome extension store or the Mozilla Firefox extension market. They are pretty easy to find and there are many good ones so I will give you a link to choose from in the Syllabus.

REALLY COOL FLASH GAME

I have also linked to a really cool flash game, which is going to help you in rapidly understanding and retaining information. The idea is in every round you need to determine the most recent bubble on the screen.

This is easy at first, but over time, you are going to have to learn to determine a lot of information quickly. If you try to do this without using saccades and scanning your eyes, you will inevitably fail. However, if you use saccades, you will see it is very quick to determine the new bubble.

The more you play this game, maybe 10 minutes a day, the quicker you will become at recognizing how much information is in each saccade.

This is a cool skill by the way, and you will notice when getting off the subway and you are looking for which exit to take, you can use saccades. You can quickly determine the destination of each exit. It is a cool trick, so try out the game.

HOMEWORK

Check the Syllabus for homework assignments and recommended supplementary materials.

Chapter 20: Improving Your Eye Span: Wider Saccades

Chapter Overview

Now that we have learned to read with saccades, we are going to expand our focal range (or eye span) to be more effective. At the speed we are performing saccades, we can make dramatic increases in our overall reading speed simply by minimizing the number of "columns" we need to make on a page.

This chapter also contains a number of exercises for improving your focal span, which can be found in the supplementary materials. For students who have been diligently working on the other games, they can switch up their routine and work on these new games. If you have not been doing the work, do not jump to these exercises until you see significant improvement in the previous games and exercises.

Essential Speed Reading Skill – Improve Your Focal Eye Span

One of the essential speed reading skills when reading in saccades is to improve your focal eye span. We can train the eye to have a wider span even if only by a little bit, and to catch more words with every saccade.

We are going to check out a few exercises now that will help us develop this skill.

Only replace or stop practicing the old exercises if you have seen significant improvements.

There is another piece of homework for you to practice 10 minutes a day just like all the other exercises. It is going to improve your eye span and make it a little bit wider. Now, when Anna told me to do this, I did not pay attention, and I really wish I had.

If you improve your eye span gradually, even gradually, you will see that you have to make fewer saccades. If you can cut one saccade out, it is going to increase your reading speed dramatically. So put in the time. I know these games seem like they do not make a huge difference, but you will notice a tremendous increase in your skill.

EYE SPAN EXERCISE

The basic idea here is to train ourselves to look in the middle of the block.

Then, as we become better and better at seeing with our peripheral vision, we can expand the block and try to remember what was in every one of these items.

Over time, you should see a dramatic improvement in your peripheral vision, and that is what we are going for.

Once you get bored of that, you can check out another link for Shultz tables, and this is a little bit more of a challenge. You will see that the columns are very, very wide apart. You can adjust them, but no matter what, this will really, really push the limits of your peripheral vision, if you find that the other exercise is a little bit too boring for you.

HOMEWORK

Check the Syllabus for Recommended Supplementary Materials

CHAPTER 21: MORE EFFICIENT SACCADES

CHAPTER OVERVIEW

We are continuing with our practice of saccades. This chapter helps us avoid one of the mistakes beginners make - wasted space and inefficiency.

For students who have mastered the "Camera Mind" exercise, this chapter also provides a much more challenging game, which you can use to replace it in your daily training regimen. It is linked in the Syllabus.

CRITICAL MISTAKE

Before we wrap up with saccades, I just want to take one minute to talk about a critical mistake that many people make. Sometimes you may notice that you start your saccades on the first word and end them on the last word in a line. If you are doing this, you are wasting precious eye span on either side reading white space.

As my father always jokingly told me, "you have to make sure you are reading the black stuff, not the white stuff." Do not start your saccades at the beginning and end them at the very end. Start them one word in and end them one word in. If you imagine your three columns, you are starting in the middle of each of the three columns.

| 1 | 2 | 3 |

cret agent in more decisions than we could imagine. It even helps us decide whom to date—and, ultimately, whom to marry. Let me describe an experiment that explored just this subject.

As students hurried around MIT one cold weekday, I asked some of them whether they would allow me to take their pictures for a study. In some cases, I got disapproving looks. A few students walked away. But most of them were happy to participate, and before long the card in my digital camera was filled with images of smiling students. I returned to my office and printed 60 of them—30 of women and 30 of men.

The following week I made an unusual request of 25 of my undergraduates. I asked them to pair the 30 photographs of men and the 30 of women by physical attractiveness (matching the men with other men, and the women with other women). That is, I had them pair the Brad Pitts and the George Clooneys of MIT, as well as the Woody Allens and the Danny De-Vitos (sorry, Woody and Danny). Out of these 30 pairs, I selected the six pairs—three female pairs

This way, you have to make fewer saccades, three instead of four in this case, and you will notice that you are getting the information in much quicker.

LEVEL 2 SHORT TERM MEMORY & SPAN GAME

If you have not advanced in the past exercises, do not move on to this one just yet. If you have, however, and you are seeing real progress, try this game out. The objective here is to try to remember all of the items in ascending order and then click them in that order. They will add numbers as you go along and thus you are not only testing your peripheral vision, you are actually also testing you are ability to store memories rapidly.

Give it a try. It gets really tough really fast.

HOMEWORK

Check the Syllabus for homework assignments and recommended supplementary materials.

SECTION 6: LET'S SPEED THINGS UP!

CHAPTER 22: SPEED TRAINING WITH A CARD

CHAPTER OVERVIEW

In this chapter, we discuss one of Anna's best techniques for helping you progress in your speed reading.

ANOTHER GREAT TRICK FROM ANNA

It is time for another one of Anna's great tricks. You see, many speed readers will tell you to use a pen or finger to follow along with the text at the speed you wish to read. This sets you up for failure, because it gives you the opportunity not only to do short, small saccades, but also to jump back on the text.

This is the enemy of speed, and it allows you to maintain very, very bad habits. While you are learning, here is an important rule:

NEVER, EVER, EVER GO BACK ON THE TEXT!

That's right. Never, ever, ever go back on the text, unless it is *absolutely* necessary, and even then, you can only go back when you have finished the entire chapter, and reviewed all of your markers.

It will be unpleasant. It will itch, it will burn, and it will drive you crazy not to go back, but you have to break this habit. This is a game-changer. **You must get over the psychological notion that you can always go back if you drift off or lose your focus**. That fallback, the metaphorical net under the tightrope, is going to limit your learning and keep you from giving your full focus.

You have to push yourself – to up the stakes, if you will. Therefore, to break this habit, we train with a card, usually an index card or something that covers up the entire page, and we cover the material that we have already read. The card goes not on the bottom, but on the top; as we go along, we are reading the line below the card.

This is great, because it prevents us from jumping back. It adds that level of friction and forces us to push forward. Furthermore, our peripheral vision is going to distract us inevitably. It is better that it distract us with what is to come rather than what we have already read. This is great for reading paper books. However, what about tablets, computers, and phones? Fortunately, most of these devices can be configured to have a "continuous scroll" effect, allowing you to use the top of the screen as if it were a card. Once you have read something, simply scroll so that it is no longer visible on the screen. Do not worry; we will be covering how to set up your devices for speed reading in depth a little bit later.

Get a card, or fold a piece of paper in half or in quarters so that it covers your reading material, and start using it from the top of the page, covering what you have already read.

HOMEWORK

Check the Syllabus for homework assignments and recommended supplementary materials.

CHAPTER 23: TRAINING AT THE SPEED YOU WISH TO READ

CHAPTER OVERVIEW

In this chapter, we apply the methodology of "Progressive Overload" to reading. We outline the progressively more difficult phases of speed, and explain why this approach is superior to others used to teach speed reading. This is by far the most challenging and frustrating portion of the course, but do not lose sight of the big picture!

PUSHING THE BOUNDARIES

Many speed reading courses encourage you to read at the fastest pace you can currently understand, and then improve your speed from there. This is actually a terrible way to learn, because you simply will not push the boundaries of your understanding or subvocalization far enough. When I learned this skill, Anna and I sat for weeks, and she pushed the card *for* me.

Every time in the beginning, I would look up and say, "Anna I can't go that fast. I didn't understand anything." She told me, "That is fine. For now, it is better to push yourself and not understand anything. Let your comprehension catch up to the speed you are trying to read."

Now, in order to avoid the complete frustration of zipping the card down the page, we are going to do this in phases.

We are going to start by moving the card down the page at a rate of 15 to 30 seconds per page, on a standard 9 by 6 novel. If you are using other materials, simply count the average number of words in a line, and the average number of lines, and then multiply them. Yes, 15 to 30 seconds, is extremely fast.

It puts you at a speed of about 600 to 1200 words per minute. Eventually, the upper range is the hoped for goal. I personally read about 800 to 1200 words a minute, depending on the level of comprehension I need. The technique here is not to speed up your reading to match your comprehension, but just the opposite.

You want to try to input at the speed you desire during the phase you are currently in, and let your comprehension catch up to that speed.

Trust me on this much: you have to push yourself a lot. You are going to feel that you are not getting anything out of the text, and that is okay. That means you are pushing yourself.

It is quite similar in this regard to weight lifting, where athletes push themselves all the way to the point where their muscles are failing. Only at that point is the body being challenged to grow. Since you don't have someone there as I did to watch your eyes and make sure that you are being true to saccades, or to move the card at the appropriate speed, you are going to rely (at least partially) on a great tool called Spreeder. Referenced in the PDF Syllabus, Spreeder is going to allow you to copy and paste text, specify the speed, and the width of the column or saccade, and it is just going to flash the text right out to you. This is a great way to improve, but make sure that you are not exclusively using Spreeder. Let's not forget the importance of saccades, which Spreeder does not teach us.

Sometimes, it is important to return to normal text and to use your card, so you are building *all* of the proper habits and skills, of course.

As I said, we recommend progressing in the gradual stages. For the purpose of practice only, you are allowed to go back after you have read the entire page or even a few pages, and check the level of comprehension to see how much detail you retained.

Now, I think it goes without saying, but remember to create markers during these practice sessions. Once you have an acceptable amount of detail, even the minimum of 50 to 60 percent of the details, move on. This will probably be about 5 to 10 sessions of 10 minutes for each phase. That is to say, this could take a few weeks to learn.

Do not get hung up on having perfect comprehension. Right now, we are trying to break the sound barrier. Improved comprehension will come with time and practice.

I also want you to think about how much detail you actually remember the week after you read with a subvocalization method. Chances are, your comprehension is going to improve, so do not worry about having 100%. 60 to 70% is more than enough for most purposes.

PHASE 1

In Phase 1, I want you to read at a rate of about 250 words per minute on Spreeder, or slightly over one minute per page on a standard novel. You probably already read this fast, but I want you to focus in doing it in saccades. Try to absorb the entire saccade as once.

"The quick brown fox" becomes one symbol, one mental marker that comes into your consciousness.

PHASE 2

For Phase 2, we are going to try 350 words per minute, or slightly under one minute per page. This is not pushing yourself too much, but we want to go in phases, so you do not get completely frustrated here.

PHASE 3

For Phase 3, I want you to try 500 words per minute on Spreeder, or less than 40 seconds per page.

I am going to remind you again, make sure you are doing a little bit of Spreeder, and a little bit of reading actual text, or reading on your iPad or Kindle.

PHASE 4

For Phase 4, I want you to do 700 words a minute on Spreeder, or less than 30 seconds per page.

PHASE 5

For Phase 5, I want you to push it to the limit. Try to go for a 1000 words a minute on Spreeder, which is more or less 15 seconds per page. I am at this level. Unfortunately, I have been a bit too busy to break 1,000 words - and if you are like me, you may not see a practical reason to do so, either.

However, this is something you can always come back to, and you can always improve your speed. You will probably hit a hard limit of about 1,500. Anything above 1,500 generally requires techniques that are more advanced and those techniques are not mentioned in this book.

Another very important thing in this phase is to push as fast as you can go.

> PUSH YOURSELF FASTER
> Anna will not be there to push for you!

Really and honestly - you absolutely must push yourself here. I cannot emphasize that enough.

You are going to plateau, probably between 700 and 1000 words per minute, and that is perfect for now. We can always come back later and improve your skills, with further practice and minor tweaks. As a side note, again, I want to stress this is going to be extremely, extremely frustrating in the beginning. You will feel that you do not even have time for your eyes to focus, much less read or comprehend the material. That is a good thing. No matter what you do, do not slow down. I hope you find solace in the words of Mario Andretti, a very famous Ferrari Formula 1 driver. He said,

"IF EVERYTHING SEEMS UNDER CONTROL,

YOU ARE NOT GOING FAST ENOUGH."

In time, your comprehension will catch up to the speed that we are having you read at in each of the phases. You should continue reaching the chapters, even while you progress through these phases, because it is going to take a few weeks, for you to see dramatic improvement here.

The next chapters also contain tips and tricks to make the process easier, and make your progression through the stages a lot less painful.

HOMEWORK

Check the Syllabus for homework assignments and recommended supplementary materials.

CHAPTER 24: SPEED TIP: TRICKING YOUR BRAIN INTO SPEEDING UP

CHAPTER OVERVIEW

In this Chapter, we examine a neat "hack" that Anna teaches for overcoming the frustration and overwhelming speed when switching to a new, faster, phase.

JUMPING FROM ONE PHASE TO THE NEXT

If you are pushing yourself as hard as you should be, you are going to suffer at the first portion of a new phase when jumping from one phase to the next. The difference between 700 words per minute and 500 words per minute, for example, is a pretty dramatic one. To overcome this, we use a cool little mental hack that Anna taught me.

We take our trusty card, and we move it along the page extremely quickly, more than double the speed at which we are trying to read. At the upper levels, this can mean that we are moving the card from the top of the page to the bottom in less than five seconds!

Now, we do this three times, and each time, we try to catch as much on the page, using saccades and our good habits, as we possibly can. Perhaps we focus on the left side for one pass, the middle one the second pass and the right side on the third pass.

We should be able to catch a few familiar words, maybe titles or numbers, but ultimately you should not expect to catch much of anything at this pace. However, you can kill two birds with one stone if you want, and do this at the same time as your pre-reading.

Now, when we slow down to our challenge speed, which felt so fast before, we are able to speed up and meet it. This is similar to the psychological effect of things feeling very light after lifting something very heavy. It is a cool little mental hack, and it tricks your brain into thinking it is not nearly as fast, relatively. You can use it anytime you are struggling to keep pace. Try this and add it to your other skills to be practiced.

HOMEWORK

Check the Syllabus for homework assignments and recommended supplementary materials.

CHAPTER 25: CREATING MARKERS AT SPEED

CHAPTER OVERVIEW

This chapter addresses some of the challenges students face when creating markers at speed

CHALLENGE – CREATING MARKERS AT SPEED

One of the biggest challenges our students often face is one of creating markers at speed. When we speed read, we use marker skills slightly differently from the way we create generic markers to remember things. This is because at the speed we are covering concepts, it can be challenging and slow you down.

So, how do we apply the concept of markers to speed reading, given the rapid pace?

First of all we usually only have 1 or 2 markers per paragraph. Unless and until the images start popping up in our heads automatically (which should happen with prolonged time and practice), we do not try to create these markers in real-time when we read the paragraph, because this way, we would start switching tasks.

Instead, we pause after each paragraph and try to remember what we read, for one or two seconds. That is usually enough to create markers, and even to link them up. As you remember from earlier on in the book, we are creating efficiency by breaking up the 3 stages of memory, and this is a perfect example of it in practice.

The general ideas of the paragraph make the markers. In the beginning, while we are still practicing, we may have to start with very simple markers that are not very lively and have limited detail. Then, we try to remember everything in the paragraph that adds information to the main idea, and visualize it as a detail of the marker.

One technique that Lev likes to use is assigning an "emotional color" of the paragraph as a marker. Red can represent anger, for example, and blue can represent calm or resolution. Emotional colors are the types of simple, easy-to-generate markers we make in the beginning. The markers should eventually start to become more and more detailed with practice.

Like I mentioned earlier, with time you will become faster and faster at creating the markers and it will become second nature. At that point, your brain will most likely create markers "on the fly" as you read, or at the very least, it will become second nature to assign markers when you reach the end of the paragraph. Of course, this takes time and practice.

For now, it is ok to take a few seconds after each paragraph to create and link markers. You are still reading much faster and with more retention than you would if you were subvocalizing!

Occasionally, you may feel that you cannot finish the paragraph, because you vocalize a word and your attention drifts off. This means that you need to stop and generate a marker. There may be several markers within a paragraph. This is perfectly OK, as long as you create an interesting and appealing animation or scheme to connect the markers.

Remember what we learned in the previous section also. When you pre-read several paragraphs in a section, your brain has some time to come up with possible markers before you actually need to use these markers. Although this may sound counter-intuitive, pre-reading speeds up marker generation and makes them available for detail collection.

ASK DR. LEV:
WHAT IF I CAN'T VISUALIZE FAST ENOUGH FOR MY READING SPEED?

Well, this is the ugly truth. Nobody can visualize fast enough for his or her reading speed. That is, of course, if we visualize each and every word. However, why would we visualize each and every word?

For some tasks, we define the goal as 100% retention. It could be learning a new language, learning a poem, or a joke, or remembering definitions. In the "Pareto" distribution of things we do, there is always this annoying 1% of tasks that requires our 99% attention. The best way to approach this within our framework is high-level visualization. Creating a single, consistent, and highly accurate scenario, and placing within this scenario detailed visualization for each and every word really works. It is also highly entertaining. Notice that middle-level visualization may also work for shorter texts. Check out middle-level visualizations on technical material. In case of detailed visualization, time and reading speed are not constraints. It is not reasonable to create such a detailed level of visualization within seconds.

For most tasks (in my case, around 80%) we can do with very few (0-5) markers per document. For example, when reading blogs, you are not expected to find A LOT of new information or generate A LOT of markers. Therefore, when reading the article, if relevant, generate a couple of markers, but when finished reading, do spend some time to link them properly. This method, which we call "hyperlinking," is harder than it seems, since you need top-notch analytical capabilities to link only the relevant information to the other relevant information. You can read blogs and some books at 2,000 wpm and generate good, properly linked markers, but your markers will cover the text sparsely (and you may miss many details).

Then, there are those tasks that are well balanced between reading speed and retention (like some *Wikipedia* articles). These tasks are those for which the original SuperLearner course was built. The idea is as follows: read the document at the regular speed (<1000 wpm) and try to generate markers as you would generate free associations. You get a lot of markers, some of them less accurate than others (based on your level of training), some of them linked (based on the content structure) some of them subvocalized (names, etc.). It is quite a mess when reading at first.

When done reading, stop and try to recreate the text using the markers you have. If you need specific details, read the text again very fast, pausing only to remember the details you need (like dates and places) with high-quality markers. Then, read a third time to unify the experience – making all the details accurate. Each time, try to recreate the article from your memory when done reading. The resulting average speed will be around 600wpm with 80% retention, but you will remember all the details you really need (dates, places, people, reasons - everything needed for a history or economics test).

Nobody I know can visualize every detail and read at his or her top speed. By choosing the right strategy, though, some of us can read VERY fast and yet remember sufficient levels of details for any purpose.

HOMEWORK

Check the Syllabus for homework assignments and recommended supplementary materials.

CHAPTER 26: TRAINING GOING FORWARD

"THERE IS NO SUBSTITUTE FOR HARD WORK."

THOMAS EDISON

Remember to practice every day and try to speed read as much as you can. If you are doing something very important for school or work, obviously, do not speed read beyond your capacity. However, if it is something nonessential, like reading *TechCrunch*, you should definitely try to speed read it.

With that, you have completed the most challenging parts of the course. Congratulations. You should practice these skills for a few weeks, or even a few months to start seeing those dramatic improvements. Sometimes, you will slip back into old habits, and I do that as well. It is perfectly understandable, and it is perfectly normal.

It takes a very long time to overcome years and years of slow reading and subvocalization. Just do not lose focus or get frustrated. If you need, you can always return to the lessons, the exercises, and the fundamentals. In fact, I strongly recommend you do so.

The remainder of this course is going to cover broader topics, including real world applications of your learning and new skills, and tailoring the skills to unique materials.

ASK DR. LEV:
AN AMAZING LIST OF SIMPLE EXERCISES

This is a short list of simple exercises you can practice anytime and anywhere. Anna gives this list only to her most prudent students.

Each exercise should take around 10 min, and you can practice it daily if you want. Alternatively, you can choose a weekly subject and focus on it for a whole week.

- Mindful memorization: listen to your surroundings and try to remember names and numbers from the first time you hear them.
- Read and remember 5 cool facts from *Wikipedia*: people, dates, new words, physics/math constants.
- Read a page and imagine how you will make it into a movie. Try to be creative and make the movie as fun as possible.
- Learn 5 words from any foreign language.
- Watch a *TED* Talk or TV series and make transcript for it from your memory. Repeat until you are happy with the result.
- Try to visualize someone you used to know well, but have not met for along time. Try to fill in as many details of their life as you can from your memory.
- Try to generate at least 5 associations for every piece of information you want to memorize. See if you can successfully recreate all 5 associations after some time. This will teach you of your personal style.
- Look once at a landscape before you, close your eyes and try to recreate as many details as you can from your memory. Open your eyes and compare. Repeat until you feel good with the result.
- Memorize numbers of passing cars. Hint: when you get better, you may need special markers for all 2-digit numbers, for example, 00 is toilet, 33 Jesus, 45 WWII victory, etc.
- Memorize grocery lists and to do's, try not to look at your calendar.
- Keep a journal of your reading: how much, what, when, and what you still remember a week after.
- Select an object, any object and write down 20 ways it can be used.

HOMEWORK

Practice <u>all</u> of the skills you've acquired thus far – any games you have not yet mastered, pre-reading, saccades, Spreeder, and using a card. Ask questions in the online group if you are having difficulty!

Check the Syllabus for homework assignments and recommended supplementary materials.

SECTION 7: SYSTEMS FOR CREATING AND MAINTAINING LONG-TERM MEMORIES

CHAPTER 27: MIND MAPPING

Another great skill that many SuperLearners use is called mind mapping. Mind mapping is drawing out a neural network of new ideas, concepts, and details. I will give you a link to an article about it with some visual mind maps you can check out yourself.

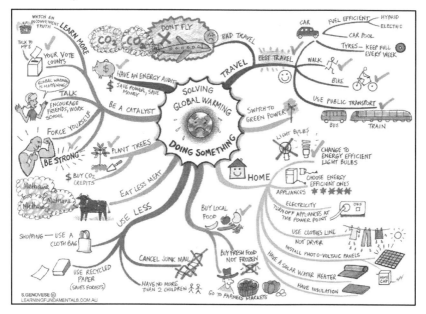

What is great about mind mapping is that it allows us to create these neural connections, and since we have already built a system where we are encoding details to get back to the main concept from the bottom up, it is very easy for us to translate that into mind maps. Mind maps have many benefits over notes, because they are visual and they allow you to show the neural connections right on paper.

It is a lot better than an outline format, for example, because there is a chance that neural connections are connected in different branches of the mind map. Mind maps are kind of a very personal thing, and they work for you or they do not. If they do work, you are going to have to play with them to see the best way for you to create and use mind maps.

Suffice it to say, that mind mapping is a very effective way to take notes, learn things, and store information for recall. If the information is too dense to remember all the details, or is too broad, mind maps organize the information in recognizable branches creating a visual picture of the information. There is a lot of great software out there for iPads and iPhones and even desktop apps to make mind maps.

You should explore and understand how mind maps fit into your own SuperLearning tool kit.

HOMEWORK

Check the Syllabus for homework assignments and recommended supplementary materials.

CHAPTER 28: MEMORY PALACES

Another very effective tool for storing and remembering information that we have SuperLearned is a technique called memory palaces. Memory palaces are imaginary buildings or structures that you create in your mind to fill and populate with detailed memories. Each story or piece of information is represented by an imaginary physical object, which is then placed in a specific area, whether it is on the ground, on a bookshelf, on the counter, in the cupboard, or dangling from the lamp. The areas where memories can be stored are called "loci," and they become anchor points. The core of the technique involves using your imagination to walk through this familiar area in a linear fashion, making sure not to cross your own path. As you go through the memory journey, you place objects in memorable areas.

> Memory palaces are imaginary buildings where we store our memories as marker objects.

I used to be very ambivalent about memory palaces, and I originally shied away from teaching too much about them. I was too lazy to invest the time in creating my own memory palaces, and so I would store my visual markers haphazardly without any order or organization. However, the more I researched and interacted with many experts on memory palaces, the more I realized that this technique is actually used by each and every memory athlete, without exception. This is for a couple of reasons.

Number 1, our brains are extremely effective at remembering where things are and visualizing them. This is related to the evolutionary skills we talked about earlier. If you remember exactly where the berry tree is in a massive field, or exactly where you buried your winter food supply, that can be a huge survival advantage.

> Our brains are extremely effective at remembering the locations of things.

This effect is so powerful that I bet that if you close your eyes right now, you can tell me exactly where the shampoo and conditioner bottles are in your shower. You can probably even tell me what order they are in! This is pretty amazing, and your brain does it *naturally*.

Number 2, this technique is very effective at helping us index events. We can remember events in chronological order, which is important for things like memorizing speeches. We can even remember things in even reverse order, if we go through our memory journey backwards.

In fact, this technique is so effective that it has been used for thousands of years, ever since the Fifth Century B.C. The legend goes that the Greek Poet Simonides was at a banquet hall crowded with people, and left for a few minutes only to find the banquet hall had collapsed. There were no other survivors, and there was no way to identify the crushed casualties - or even know where they were.

In that moment, Simonides realized that if he closed his eyes, he could remember exactly where each person had been sitting, even though he had not really been paying attention over the wine, food, and merriment of the banquet. He was able to take each hysterical relative to the exact place where his or her loved one had been sitting.

In this moment, the memory palace was born, and for thousands of years after that (until the popularity of the printing press), memory palaces were used to memorize huge volumes of information. In fact, researchers have determined that the entire works of Homer, Plato, and Socrates were likely committed to memory using memory palaces, and only later written down.

So, how do you take advantage of this technique? The first step is to create at least one, but probably a few more, empty palaces.

The palace can be your childhood home, a building once seen, or any building you make up. In fact, most people who use this technique have many different memory palaces for different types of memories, for example one for your Spanish vocabulary, one for personal information such as birthdays and credit card numbers, and so on. Once you create the palace, you need to clear off shelves and make space for new objects. Then, it is time to start practicing placing your markers in strategic areas.

Now, I want to take a quick second to say that memory palaces are not used for everything. For example, it would be extremely difficult to use the Loci method and walk through an imaginary house while we are speed-reading, and so we cannot use this technique while we read. We just have to link the markers as we go.

Memory palaces are great for memorizing stories, order of events, lists of items, and things like that, but only when we have time to carefully populate a memory palace. Therefore, if you read something, for example, and want to store the content into a memory palace, that is something you should do at the end of the chapter, not while you are reading.

There is a great deal of amazing resources involving memory palaces, and they go into much more detail than I can in just one chapter.

First, I am going to refer you to a *TED* Talk by the U.S. memorization champion Joshua Foer, where he explains how people are able to memorize 34 decks of playing cards back to back using memory temples/palaces.

Next, I am going to link you to Foer's book, *Moonwalking with Einstein*, which I strongly recommend as homework for this course.

Finally, I am going to link you to a course on *Udemy*, a blog, book, and podcast by Dr. Anthony Metivier. Anthony is a friend and fellow *Udemy* instructor. He has made an entire career out of teaching the Magnetic Memory Method, a system based on creating and adapting memory palaces. He has written a number of books, released a number of courses, and is a very active blogger and podcaster on the subject. Actually, Anthony is the one who convinced me to invest in my own memory palaces. He continues to help me develop this skill as time goes on.

These days, I use the technique for even the simplest of things. One little hack I really like is to adapt the technique to my meditation. As a beginner in meditation, my brain immediately calls up all of the things I need to remember to do, and has some of it is best ideas when I am trying to concentrate on meditation. The standard practice is to observe the thoughts and let them pass, which I do. However, before I let these strokes of inspiration pass, I make a quick mental marker. For example, if I want to remember to post a poll on the SuperLearners *Facebook* group, I create a mental marker of *Facebook*, a voting poll and a screenshot. I place the marker on an imagined bookshelf. This allows me to move on and let the thought go with ease.

By the time I finish my normal meditation session, I may have four or five reminders. I have been amazed by how well the Loci method works. Even a month later, I remember all of these markers, where they are on the bookshelf and what each one of them represents, even without using the correct technique of walking through a palace.

I recently was interviewed by someone who read Joshua Foer's book and had done the practice exercise of memorizing a random grocery list. Five years later, he was able to remember over half of the list the Foer details in the book. Totally amazing!

Your homework is to check out the supplementary materials and memorize your entire to-do list or grocery-shopping list using loci and visual markers. Get funky and outrageous with them - you can turn "email boss" into a picture of Bowser, the big boss from Mario brothers, sitting at a computer, or you can turn "wash the car" into a picture of two bikini clad beauties sponging your car. Because you have become so skilled at creating detailed and creative markers by now, it should be no problem. Just place them in a memory palace.

Do not make the mistake I made for years and stubbornly neglect the memory palace technique! It can make a massive difference in your memory capacity.

HOMEWORK

Check the Syllabus for homework assignments and recommended supplementary materials.

Create your first memory palace and fill it with your to-do or grocery list

CHAPTER 29: NUMBER MEMORIZATION SYSTEM

If you checked out that supplementary *TED* Talk about advanced memory, then you already know a bit about what we are going to discuss here. What we want to do when we have to memorize large sequences of numbers is to create detailed visual markers for each number. It is no different from markers when you read.

You can transform these long numbers into stories, and memorize longer strings of information much more permanently than you could otherwise. One method is to build a marker for each number. I will give you my own system and my own markers, but you should think about making your own if they are more emotionally relevant for you than mine are.

As with any marker, the more ridiculous these markers are the better it is going to be when you are remembering strings of numbers.

Zero is a bagel.	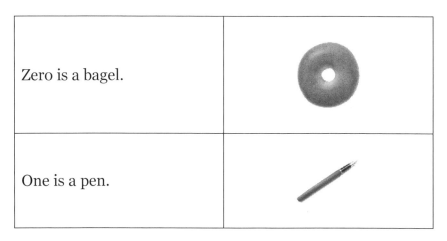
One is a pen.	

Two is a broken heart,	
Three is, of course, a butt.	
Four is a chair	
Five is a unicycle	
Six is a broken pair of glasses	

Seven is a cliff	
Eight is a racetrack	
Nine is a tadpole	

From there, you can remember a number like 867-5309. The number becomes the story:

The racetrack had a pair of broken glasses on it. The driver swerved to avoid them, and he ran off a cliff. The man on the unicycle in the crowd was shocked, and he fell on his butt swallowing the tadpole he was balancing on his tongue.

This is a truly ridiculous story. There is no way that I am going to forget the number 867-5309.

If you want to get really advanced with this, I have provided a link that explains an even more sophisticated system known as the Major System. This system allows you to encode each one of these digits not into pictures, but actually into sounds.

Numeral	Associated Consonants	Mnemonic
0	s, z, soft c	"z" is the first letter of zero. The other letters have a similar sound.

1	t, d, th	t & d have one downstroke and sound similar (some variant systems omit "th")
2	n	n has two downstrokes
3	m	M has three downstrokes and looks like a "3" on its side
4	r	last letter of four, also 4 and R are almost mirror images of each other
5	l	L is the Roman Numeral for 50. Also, if you hold up your **l**eft hand, your thumb and index fingers form an L, and you have five fingers.
6	j, sh, ch (as in cheese), soft g	a script j has a lower loop / g is almost a 6 rotated
7	k, c (as in cat), hard g, ch (as in loch), q	capital K "contains" two sevens (some variant systems include "ng" /ŋ/.)
8	f, v	script f resembles a figure-8. V sounds similar. (v is a voiced f)
9	p, b	p is a mirror-image 9. b sounds similar and resembles a 9 rolled around.
Unassigned	Vowel sounds, w,h,y	These can be used anywhere without changing a word's number value

Now, I know what you are thinking, sounds are not the best way to memorize. However, when you add those sounds up, they actually become pictures.

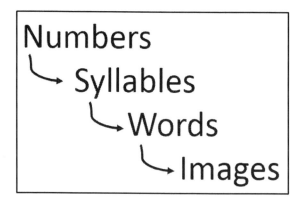

For example, 42 becomes the word rain. Whenever I think of rain in one of my stories, I know that the number 42 is there.

This is awesome if you have to remember lots and lots of numbers, for example, hundreds of numbers in a row, or the passcode to ten different safes. Personally, I have actually never needed this skill, and so I have never invested in actually learning it. If it is something that you need, you should definitely check it out, though, because it is going to be a lot more effective and efficient than memorizing the digits with one marker per digit.

HOMEWORK

Check the Syllabus for homework assignments and recommended supplementary materials.

CHAPTER 30: CHUNKING

Another cool and important SuperLearning skill is chunking. You see, most of our brains can only remember sequences of three to four numbers. You can look up a random number generator online and see how many numbers you can remember. From there, you know into what size, or how small the chunks need to be broken.

If you have ever wondered why phone numbers have the dash in the middle, this is because the average person can remember four numbers. Therefore, remembering a phone number, if you do not have our number memorization system, can be difficult. Three digits for the area code, seven digits for the number – that is ten digits, if they were strung together.

However, to remember (408) 867-5309 in three separate chunks is pretty easy. Now, if you are using short pieces of information, or information that we do not have a system for, like our numbering coding system, and especially if it is just short-term memory that you need it, the chunking system is very good.

For example if you take pieces of information such as brown dog, tall fence, lost Frisbee, those chunks are much easier to remember than the brown dog saw the tall fence where the Frisbee was lost.

Chunking also works for stories. It works for many different things. In fact, this is why we told you to try to remember four details per marker instead of five or seven details per marker.

Play around with chunking. Try to remember that four is a significant number for the number of details we can remember, the number of numbers we can remember, and so on.

HOMEWORK

Check the Syllabus for homework assignments and recommended supplementary materials.

SECTION 8: GOOD LEARNING HABITS

CHAPTER 31: SLEEPING AND LEARNING

Sleep is a very broad topic, and it is a little bit out of the purview of this course. However, I want to talk about it a little bit, because in the past many researchers did not quite understand why we sleep. They are now starting to understand that sleep is actually a critical process of learning.

> Quality sleep is more important for SuperLearners

During sleep, researchers believe that we move things from our short-term memory into our longer-term memory. More importantly, a recent study from the University of Rochester determined that sleep was an essential function in clearing out toxic metabolic waste from the brain. Because we are SuperLearners, it is logical that we are creating metabolic waste at a much faster rate. This explains some of the exhaustion you might experience.

> Memory naps allow your brain to clear the buffer of your short-term memory

For example, when I started really accelerating my learning pace after Anna's course, I found that I was completely exhausted after most sessions. I could read for about an hour to an hour and a half, and then I needed a 10 to 15-minute nap.

You might have the same experience. I know many SuperLearners do. Do not fight it. Most importantly, do not try to compensate with caffeine. A power nap is always better for learning.

Depriving your sleep is not the way to accelerate your learning pace. If you can get into sleep hacking, or get into the habit of power naps of about 22 to 24 minutes, that is the best way to do it.

Any more than 24 minutes, you will actually enter into a deeper sleep, and will wake up groggier. Any less usually does not do much, although sometimes a 10 to 15-minute nap can be very effective. Try it out and play with it. Just remember that sleep is a very, very essential component of learning.

Again, it is very similar to going to the gym and lifting weights. If you are not eating enough, you certainly will not get bigger, stronger, or healthier. So remember, sleep is a huge component of your learning process.

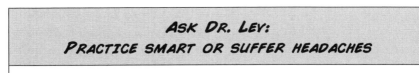

ASK DR. LEV:
PRACTICE SMART OR SUFFER HEADACHES

Some of our students occasionally report headaches. There are many sorts of headaches, but they have one thing in common: wrong technique.

There are many common ideas between going to the gym and training your brain. Just as bad practices in the gym can cause backaches and orthopedic damage, bad practices with your brain can cause headaches or eyestrain, etc.

The first thing you should do when training your brain is to rest regularly. Adopt 5 minutes of rest for every 15 minutes of work or similar activities. When resting, close your eyes or look at far away landscapes. Do not brain-train for more than 2 hours straight, even if you do take the short breaks. Coffee helps, as long as you do not drink too much of it. Make sure you drink a lot of water.

The next thing to watch is your breathing technique. Your brain should get enough oxygen. Take several long deep breathes before and after each article. See this video for an explanation: https://jle.vi/breath

You may want to practice breathing exercises like pranayama-yoga see this video: http://jle.vi/sby

I use my own breathing methodology similar to this article, adapting the specific breathing routine to my current mood. Whatever you choose, it is important to get enough oxygen to your brain.

Just like any other activity, when you are SuperLearning, you want to have ergonomic posture, a healthy diet, and a good amount of sleep. This is basic. Some people get it; others do not. We had no luck teaching people good habits, so we trust your better judgement.

Some of the recommendations are more specific. When practicing visualization, always try to make up funny stuff. Creative markers are refreshing for your brain and your willpower. Do not fixate: try to move quickly from one marker to another. Make the markers highly active in space: they may rotate, get smaller and larger, morph, collide, and do things that cartoon characters do.

By far the most challenging practice is saccade reading. If your eyes hurt, you are doing something wrong. Stop immediately, close your eyes, and think about how you can improve your practice. The eye muscles are very similar to other muscles in your body: what is hard now may be easy in a couple of days. Saccade reading assumes eye "jumping" is done in a controlled fashion, with a small overlaps on the horizontal field of view between jumps. Before you are ready to jump, move continuously. Only when the continuous movement gets too slow for you, do you then start jumping. At the beginning, the control is not that good, and your eyes may point to places in the line you did not intend to look at. Do not worry, and do not try to force your eyes to move "just right." They will adapt themselves. Do not fixate too long on any point in space; allow your eyes to move and make sure to pause between paragraphs.

Proper brain training is like magic, and may transform a healthy brain into a super-powered one, or heal an injured brain and even eliminate boredom. Bad practice causes headaches. So do practice smartly and be mindful of your body.

HOMEWORK

Check the Syllabus for homework assignments and recommended supplementary materials.

Chapter 32: The Proper Learning Environment

Another thing I think we should really talk about is the idea of state-based learning. There is a lot of interesting research about this, and you have probably experienced it yourself. I, for one, in college would always study with classical music, and I found that without the same music during exams, I really struggled.

Studies have also shown that if you chew gum, both while studying and while taking an exam, (or even if you are drunk while studying during the exam), you retain the information better. We can hack this, turn it on its head, and strategize that if you are not going to be able to have music when you need to use the information, it is better not to study with music.

Likewise, if you work in a crowded open office, it is better to study in a coffee shop or cafe where there is noise and distractions. State-based learning is a really, powerful thing, and so we should be very cognitive of how we are learning and in what environment.

On that note, we also want to think about designing our environment both for actual use of the information and for learning itself. If we can avoid noise in both of those situations, that is great. If we can avoid laying down or sitting down on our bed, that is another great way to retain alertness. Personally, I work at a standing desk, and I will be happy to link you to an article on how to build your own standing desk.

This creates alertness, makes sure that I am in the proper environment, and keeps my body active. Another important thing is having light. If you have the right color of light at the right time of day, it is going to tell your body what should be happening. Bright, white, sunlight color is going to tell you to be alert, whereas if you are using yellow lights, it is going to tell your body that it needs to start being tired.

This is why many companies use fluorescent white lights in their offices, *not* because it is more pleasant on the eyes. Also, make sure that you have enough oxygen flowing through and fresh air. Oxygen is a stimulant for the brain, much like coffee, and so having a houseplant or opening windows can really affect your learning experience.

A NOTE ON COFFEE

Coffee is actually a great way to learn if it is not abused or used in place of sleep. Coffee is a great stimulant, but it is inferior to tea in its brain-boosting power. This is because tea contains a compound called L-Theanine. L-Theanine is a naturally occurring nootropic or "smart drug," and produces a pronounced calm and focus. Another great nootropic you can look into is a ginseng and gingko biloba mix. These compounds each act a lot like attention deficit medication, opening up receptors and hormones in the brain, like serotonin, which are going to allow your brain to absorb information and create an interest and desire to learn.

ASK DR. LEV:
"FLOW" OR "THE ZONE" – AND HOW TO GET THERE

To enjoy work and learning, to enjoy life itself, I rely heavily on something called "flow." The feeling is very pleasant, invigorating, and positive. Here is the definition from *Wikipedia*:

> *Flow is the mental state of operation in which a person performing an activity is fully immersed in a feeling of energized focus, full involvement, and enjoyment in the process of the activity. In essence, flow is characterized by complete absorption in what one does. Proposed by Mihály Csíkszentmhályi, this positive psychology concept has been widely referenced across a variety of fields. According to Csikszentmhalyi, flow is completely focused*

motivation. It is a single-minded immersion and represents perhaps the ultimate experience in harnessing the emotions in the service of performing and learning. In flow, the emotions are not just contained and channeled, but positive, energized, and aligned with the task at hand. The hallmark of flow is a feeling of spontaneous joy, even rapture, while performing a task although flow is also described as a deep focus on nothing but the activity – not even oneself or one's emotions.

It is commonly accepted that one of the ways to reach "flow" is by having perfect match between the personal skill and the task at hand. Most people simply cannot generate this "perfect match" most of the time, so it remains a domain of artists, sportsmen, and monks.

Since I became what we call in this course a "SuperLearner" I noticed that I seldom get bored and often get deeply and emotionally involved in my work. Why does it happen? Well, previously, 90% of my work I was doing something that I was overqualified for. When the job gets boring, we get relaxed, and the brain partially "shuts down" into some sort of autopilot mode. Simply speeding up the simple parts generates enough load on the brain to disable this shutdown mechanism. If anything, the brain becomes overly active, and free to enter the "flow" state.

The next step is activating measurable goals (read the articles, write the post/code/presentation, generate an idea) and use creativity (visualization, associations etc.) in order to achieve those goals. Fortunately, this is exactly what the SuperLearner is trained to do with pre-reading!

Being a SuperLearner is only a part of the package. We have a full set of tricks to speed-up everyday tasks – computer usage and mobile usage generate meaningful communication. We speed up all activities to the point that they stop being boring, and generate the "flow!"

> Being a SuperLearner not only allows us to generate funny water-cooler discussions or find the perfect job, it also enables deep satisfaction from our work and from everyday life.

HOMEWORK

Check the Syllabus for homework assignments and recommended supplementary materials.

Chapter 33: Long Term Storage: Maintaining Memories

Now, despite the fact that we have invested in building these neural connections into new information, there is still a chance that our mind will forget the information over time. The chart below shows the drop-off of memory over time. This is something that Benny Lewis talks about in his *TED* Talk.

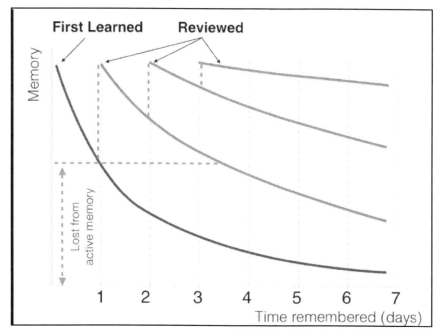

You have to refresh your knowledge and keep it relevant. Fortunately, today there are applications like that actually know this, and will remind you of the information at the scheduled times you are likely to forget it. This is called "spaced repetition," and it is one of the most powerful secret weapons for maintaining long-term memories in the SuperLearner's toolkit. In the course syllabus, you will find some videos and links instructing you on how to use a software called Anki. It's a really amazing technological innovation, because it not only has a version for anything with a screen and the free synchronization service to connect them all, but it also has great documentation, where it teaches you about the learning methodology and how to add cards with pictures, audio, other rich text, and more. The documentation will explain a bit more about how spaced repetition works, too. The creators of Anki really do a great job of documenting the process of learning with the software. They also have shared decks for just about anything you would want to learn, especially if you are looking to learn languages, which is something we will cover in another section.

I recommend Anki almost every single day, because it is a great way to review, and it takes the burden out of worrying what you are or not going to forget over time.

I am going to give you some links to Anki and other utilities but, in general, if you do not use an automatic utility, make a habit of skimming back over the text you really need to remember, after ten days, after a month, and after six months.

Play with the amount of time. When you sense you are starting to forget the information, come back, make a note of the amount of time in your specific case the information began to fade. Then the next time when you learn, remember that it is okay and it is important to revise information.

There is nothing wrong with you. Our brains just work that way.

ASK DR. LEV:
HOW MANY REPETITIONS ARE NECESSARY FOR LONG-TERM RETENTION?

Some students ask how many repetitions are required to memorize something. Long ago, I was told that seven repetitions make us remember almost anything (http://jle.vi/ro7). Now, I am ready to add some science to it. Basically, I follow the logic of this article *Wikipedia* article entitled *Spaced Repetition*: (http://jle.vi/sr).

Our neurons are hard-wired to forget something with roughly exponential speed. (http://jle.vi/forgetting).

We can fight these phenomena via various techniques.

Most of our techniques work simply because neurons work as groups, (http://jle.vi/pnas) and any new knowledge is supported by other neurons within the group. We trick the brain to include new pieces of knowledge with older and established knowledge, and ensure that we will not forget anything important. Eventually, we are left only with things that simply cannot be connected to strongly connected established neural groups: numbers, new words, names, whole new areas of knowledge. Then, we need to activate the spaced repetition approach.

We can try to check what we forget, and learn it again and again until we succeed. This method (http://jle.vi/leitner) is labor intensive, and involves checking our recall repeatedly. If we fail, we will check it more often, but if we succeed, we will need to check it much less often, until we do not need to check any more. In this approach, the frequency of repetition is governed by the amount of new data we need to learn. Computers make the job easy (using Anki or equivalent). All we need to do is create the cards with the pieces of knowledge we need to retain.

Alternatively, we may assume that all the pieces of knowledge are equally complex, like words of new language. In this case, we can calculate and time the next recall. In his seminal work, linguistics expert Paul Pimsleur (http://jle.vi/pimsleur) used 5 seconds, 25 seconds, 2 minutes, 10 minutes, 1 hour, 5 hours, 1 day, 5 days, 25 days, 4 months, and 2 years.

This is slightly more than the rule of seven, but the effect of each following repetition is reduced. Please notice that the words need to be presented in random order for the method to work.

At this point, I will refer to the original study (http://jle.vi/ebbinghaus) of the learning and forgetting curves:

> "In 1885 Ebbinghaus published his groundbreaking Über das Gedächtnis ("On Memory," later translated to English as *Memory: A Contribution to Experimental Psychology*) in which he described experiments he conducted on himself to describe the processes of learning and forgetting. Ebbinghaus made several findings that are still relevant and supported to this day. First, arguably his most famous finding is the forgetting curve. The forgetting curve describes the exponential loss of information that one has learned. The sharpest decline occurs in the first twenty minutes and the decay is significant through the first hour. The curve levels off after about one day. The learning curve described by Ebbinghaus refers to how fast one learns information. The sharpest increase occurs after the first try and then gradually evens out, meaning that less and less new information is retained after each repetition. Like the forgetting curve, the learning curve is exponential.
>
> Ebbinghaus had also documented the serial position effect, which describes how the position of an item affects recall. The two main concepts in the serial position effect are recency and primacy. The recency effect describes the increased recall of the most recent information because it is still in the short-term memory. The primacy effect better memory of the first items in a list due to increased rehearsal and commitment to long-term memory. Ebbinghaus also described the difference between involuntary and voluntary memory, the former

occurring "with apparent spontaneity and without any act of the will" and the latter being brought "into consciousness by an exertion of the will."

It is interesting to note that Ebbinghaus used to learn meaningless syllables, and he remembered the syllables that had meaning by mere chance much more than others. Moreover, even if he forgot something, he learned it easier the next time he had to re-learn it. Finally, he applied a great deal of effort to eliminate any dual coding or memorization technique from his study to preserve statistical purity. You are not studying memory curves, so you should do just the opposite: add dual coding, add meaning and memorization techniques.

I will summarize the subject as follows:

1. If you learn simple facts in an area you are familiar with, you may retain without spaced repetition.

2. If you encode the information in many forms (associations, audio, image, the way the word looks) you may need fewer repetitions.

3. For new languages or other unstructured data, you may need seven repetitions or more, with each repetition contributing less than previous.

4. If you do need spaced repetitions, it is best to use computer programs with flash cards.

HOMEWORK

Download and configure Anki. It is a must!

Check the Syllabus for homework assignments and recommended supplementary materials.

SECTION 9: APPLYING YOUR NEW SKILLS TO ANYTHING AND EVERYTHING

CHAPTER 34: TAILORING SKILLS: DENSE MATERIALS / TEXTBOOKS

If you remember the story I told you of how and when I began to learn from Anna, you will remember that I chose to take the course because I was approaching an MBA, and a particularly condensed program at an elite business school. One of the most critical things that I wanted Anna to teach me was how to learn dense materials such as statistics, finance, accounting from textbooks, using these skills.

> Pre-reading becomes more important as text complexity and density increase.

With dense materials such as textbooks, it is very important that you increase your investment in pre-reading. If there are photos in the book, use the existing photos in the textbooks as markers and store them during the pre-reading process.

If you are reading even more dense materials like law or medicine, you have to rely very heavily on creating an intense interest, and imagining of real world application. Furthermore, you need to constantly think and imagine different examples. For instance, think of the events or symptoms happening to different characters with whom you may be familiar. If you can connect the legal happenings to someone you know, or someone you know who went through them that will be a fantastic way to create interest.

Imagine you have a great aunt or uncle, for example, who had a thyroid problem discussed in your biology textbook, or a great uncle who sued the government just like in your case study. If you do this, and you create this interest during the pre-reading phase, you will find that very dense materials are much easier to get through.

ASK DR. LEV:
READING DETAIL-RICH MATERIAL

Many of our students need to learn boring, complex material rich in details. How do you remember complex statistics or medical descriptions? You break it into smaller steps, use a lot of humor, and try to keep a consistent tone in details and imagery. We teach our advanced students high-level visualization, but you can successfully remember lots of details without it. Below are examples from discussions in our *Udemy* course.

Student

So I opened up *Wikipedia* and I started to learn about GSP Belgrade.

The things I tried to remember are:

- Public Transit Company
- Created in Oct 14, 1892
- First line was a horse tram between Slavija and Terazije.
- Has 145 lines, 12 are trams, 8 are trolley bus and 125 are bus lines.
- Hours of operation are 4am to Midnight with limited night buses.
- There are about 6,200 employees
- They use about 1000 Vehicles

I have difficulty actually turning this data into images.

I can attach the Oct 14 to my mum's birthday, however I don't really know what to do with the other stats.

Any advice?

Dr. Lev:

Thank you for the question. The way to proceed is an issue of personal style. I will try to present my personal approach. Eventually, the more you know, the easier it will be to learn. Let's try to encode based on my prior knowledge:

The Belgrade GSP started to work during the Homestead Strike on Carnegie steel mill. It has

- 125 bus lines (I encode 125 as 5*5*5 and have a special marker for it, like 3 hands touching),
- 12 trams (lucky number, one more and they would hit the unlucky 13. I use a trellis for a luck symbol)
- 8 trolleys (8 looks like infinity and trolleys are infinitely cumbersome for a city).
- They are closed from Midnight to 4am (there is a 2009 movie called "4am is the new midnight").
- There are 1K vehicles (I have a special marker for a kilo).
- The number of employees in *Wikipedia* is 6166, (I have a number 666 encoded as Satan, so just remember 1 non-satanic employee).

Now if I really do not want to forget, just make up a funny story. Sometimes I actually prefer to remember information as comics:

During the Homestead Strike the workers came to your mother's home and shake hands with her 3 times. The shake was infinitely long and she was lucky when it was over. It felt like midnight in poorly rated movie and the hand was getting very heavy. Then a fourth worker came in and stood second in the row, and all 3 previous workers started growing horns.

Try to find your own personal style.

Good luck!

Student:

Can I use this exercise / method for each type of text?

I choose today the text about Adductor muscles of the hip (http://jle.vi/hip). I find it very complicated to find pictures to some words.

If I want to learn all the muscles of the adductor group:

- Adductor brevis
- Adductor longus
- Adductor magnus
- Adductor minimus
- Adductor magnus.
- Pectineus
- Gracilis
- Obturator externus

Can I use the method of markers or need I something else?

Then I tried another article: Pilates. I started with history – http://jle.vi/pilates

I took the German article. My English is not so good.

The first sentence: Joseph Hubert Pilates (1883–1967) war Turner, Taucher, Bodybuilder und Zirkusartist.

In English:

Hubert Joseph Pilates (1883-1967) was a gymnast, diver, bodybuilder and circus performer.

For me there are a lot markers in one sentence and I start to find pictures for:

- Hubert
- 1883 / 1967
- gymnast
- diver
- bodybuilder
- circus performer.

Am I on the right track?

Jonathan :

Thanks for a fantastic question, Klaus.

Let's start with the muscles of the hip. This is an extremely difficult one, but you should rely on existing knowledge to create markers. Your knowledge may differ from mine, but let me demonstrate how I might create markers.

- **Adductor brevis**
  - My mind jumps to "brevity," and I picture a scene from the movie "The Big Lebowsky" where he uses the word "brevity" – this is my marker for that word, always. It's a vivid image in my mind of the character
  - Brevity means short (brevis in Latin), and so I remember that this is shorter than the next one, adductor longus
- **Adductor longus**
  - The "long" in the name obviously gives me a marker, and I might just remember that it's the longest muscle in the leg, using the marker of the image supplied in *Wikipedia*
- **Adductor magnus**
  - Magnus means "great" in Latin, but we may not know that. I see that this muscle is very small, and I think that it must be a pretty great muscle to keep up with the other 2 longer muscles it's next to
  - I use as a marker a picture of the world's strongest man, Magnus Vermagnussen. He is very strong, and this little muscle must be too, as said above
- **Adductor minimus**
  - See similar techniques as above
- **Pectineus**
  - I think of the "pectoral" muscle, which is in a similar position to the shoulder. My marker is my pectoral muscle, which I've seen a million times, and which rotates my shoulder in just like this muscle does for the leg
  - If you need to make another marker here, that is fine. Think of something silly or outrageous, like feeding a bird out of your lap and having it "peck" you your inner leg accidentally.

- **gracilis**
  - This muscle is thin and graceful, I picture a graceful woman in a long ball dress who also looks thin
- **Obturator externus**
  - Similar methods to above

Now, that was tricky, but it should give you an idea. I am really going for "vivid" and concrete imagery, and I am trying to tack on to anything that is already part of my existing knowledge. Movies, English words, Latin words, muscles I already know – any connection I can make, I make. Now, if you covered up the labels on the muscles, I could recite the names to you because I have a silly memory or story connected to each one. I do not remember Adductor Brevis, I remember The Big Lebowsky... "So you are not into Brevity... I get that..."

Now let's talk about the Pilates question. You are definitely on the right track. This is a very information dense paragraph. I am interested in knowing how involved he was with sports and activity, given what he designed with the Pilates program, and so I would definitely make markers for Gymnast, Circus performer, bodybuilder, and probably even diver. I do not know that the dates would be that important to me – maybe just the death date. His name is pretty important, too, but I do not have a marker for Hubert, so the first thing that came to mind was the Sesame Street character "Bert" – but in a different hue, like green. It is silly, but it is a functional marker for me.

HOMEWORK

Check the Syllabus for homework assignments and recommended supplementary materials.

CHAPTER 35: TAILORING SKILLS: LEARNING LANGUAGES

Now, for learning a language, I am going to be referring you to a couple of great sites. One is the *Fluent Forever* website by Gabriel Wyner, which is an independent site that will tell you a lot about the principles of learning languages very quickly, overcoming pronunciation, vocabulary, and grammar. There are many great articles here, and Gabriel's book is one of my go-to resources for learning languages quickly and efficiently.

I am also going to refer you to Benny Lewis's site, and a podcast episode I recorded with him. Benny is the guy who gave the *TED* Talk we linked to earlier, and he has developed a "fluent in three months" methodology that helps many people overcome the barrier of learning a language.

Nonetheless, let's review some of the major talking points here involved in learning a language, just to give you a brief overview of what is going to be contained on these websites and books.

DO NOT TRANSLATE TO YOUR LANGUAGE

When applying the skills to learning new languages, there is a very important rule that differs from other information. The rule is no translating words to your native language. This is how *Rosetta Stone* works, for example, and it is for a very good reason. When you translate a word, you create one neural link to that word in your existing or native language. This is a very weak connection and it is very easy to forget. If you have ever done a Google translate on a word and forgotten it immediately thereafter, you now understand why.

Instead, you need to link it to an existing mental marker, or image, feeling or smell that is already densely built into a neural network. This way you are tapping into that network and the material stays much more relevant for your mind.

LEARNING NEW WORDS

Now for pronunciation of new words, you want to try to think of neurally linked words and sounds that you already know. For example, if we are learning Spanish and the word is bano (bathroom), try to think of a crazy situation, a very memorable one. For example, if you are trying to find the restroom in a restaurant and you have a little bit of an accident, they are likely to ban you, or bano.

Now, does this seem really silly? Of course. I understand that, but it works for improving your memorization of foreign sounds in your new language. Just remember, we are not translating here. We are linking neural points of sounds to neural points of concepts. If you have not already checked out Benny Lewis' amazing *TED* Talk, check it out.

MOTIVATION

Benny talks about the very important subject of motivation. It is something we already talked about, and so I am not going to loop over it. However, with something as complex as a language, it requires a lot of dedication. Therefore, make sure you are adhering to Malcolm Knowles' six requirements for adult learning.

Make sure you have a reason to learn the language, a pressing interest, an opportunity to practice, and that you are connecting it to your existing experiences and knowledge.

In addition to my podcast episode with Benny, I recently had the opportunity to meet a real-life polyglot. This was not someone who has intentionally studied 20 or 30 languages, but someone who was a self-proclaimed "natural" language learner. He told me how he spoke six different languages starting from the age of 5 or 6, and I immediately took the opportunity to pick his brain. I wanted to see if the approach that he'd developed, or which he believed came naturally to him, coincided with the methodologies that we've been discussing, both for regular learning, and for language learning.

Like Benny Lewis, this "natural" language learner told me that his secret was that he rarely ever learns in classes. In fact, he told me that he struggled very much to learn in a classroom setting with a textbook. He said that things did not seem real enough, and he could not extract enough meaning or really get a feel for the words he was trying to learn, this sounds familiar.

Also like Benny, the "natural" learner told me that he learned languages primarily by speaking to people, in real life situations. He would try to get by in the language or listen to people in supermarkets speaking that language. Now, what this tells me is that he is creating contextual memories and linking them to existing neural networks.

He probably already has a situation where he asks the butcher how much something costs or how much it weighs. Therefore, he is linking these new words to those existing neural networks.

This is in complete contrast to the way you learn in a class. In class, you create hypothetical scenarios such as, "I need to go to the restroom," or "Can you tell me where the library is?"

These things stand completely alone in the brain. That is probably why he (and many others) struggled so much to learn in a language class. Trying to just get by in the language and feeling around for the words, or dancing around the words that you do not know, is also a really great way to create experiential learning. Ultimately, this means that you have to get over the embarrassment and start speaking your language from day one; this is the core principle that Benny Lewis shares with all his students. The more mistakes you make, the better, as those create memorable and emotional markers by which you will remember.

For example, I will never forget the proper conjugation of the word flowers in Hebrew, because when I was young, I conjugated it incorrectly, into a completely different word, and it was an embarrassing memory. However, it helped me remember the proper conjugation of the word. Therefore, different experiences are going to be very helpful. If you are studying in a classroom, or if you are reading a textbook and passively taking in these experiences, you are not going to remember them.

Another interesting thing about this "natural" language learner was that without knowing it, he was actually abiding by most of Malcolm Knowles' six rules for adult learners. For example, he told me that it was his passion to learn languages since he was a child, trying to communicate with his grandparents, and that he takes it very, very seriously, because it is something he loves and enjoys doing. When I told him, "That is very impressive, you could probably learn 20 languages if you wanted to." He immediately replied, "Yeah, but, I don't have any use for 20 languages, and so I won't invest the time."

This shows us that having the proper motivation and the proper applicability is important in language learning, and this is something that this natural polyglot had already figured out on his own. Another interesting thing he said to me was that he writes everything down and he tries to look at pictures a lot. No surprises there!

ANKI AND LEARNING LANGUAGES

The use of images coincides with a method that I have seen for using Anki and learning languages. What many people do on Anki is actually watch a movie in a foreign language with subtitles. As they go along, the subtitles will give them context and meaning for different situations and different words.

Because Anki allows you to take screenshots and upload images, they will actually just upload that image right there and then. If you are trying to learn the word for pirate in German and you have a screenshot of Johnny Depp and the word in German below in subtitles, that gives you context and meaning, links it to your already existing knowledge about pirates, or about Johnny Depp, or anything that will draw the word closer in to that neural network.

This is an amazing tool. I have been using it myself to brush up on my language skills, and I can tell you it really, really works.

Another method advocated by Gabriel Wyner in his book Fluent Forever is to put only images and the foreign word. He puts absolutely no English on his cards, and I suggest you do the same, whichever method you use for creating Anki decks.

SPEED READING IN OTHER LANGUAGES

Now, as far as speed reading in other languages, it is going to vary a lot per language. I am told that in Chinese, Japanese and Korean, none of which I personally speak of course, speed reading is a bit more difficult as the density of meaning to eye span is already highly condensed. In German, I am told that you must focus on the end of the sentences. In Semitic languages, such as Hebrew, Turkish, Farsi, and Arabic you should focus on the centers, or the root formations of the words.

As more and more of you take this course and apply these skills to other languages, we are really looking for feedback and we hope to expand the language-learning portion. Therefore, if you figure out a different tip or trick, or you have some ideas how to speed read your native language, please let us know, and we will be adding it to the course.

HOMEWORK

Check the Syllabus for homework assignments and recommended supplementary materials.

Chapter 36: Tailoring The Skills: Never Forget A Face Or A Name

Remembering the faces and names of new people is easy if you take the right approach. Whereas most people would recommend repeating the name seven times, this is actually a mistake. As you now understand, that single neuron of information will be all alone, without any synapses connecting to it.

Instead, you should try to connect that person to another person or idea. Try to connect it to another person with the same name, or even a story you heard about someone with that same name. What is one feature that Stephanie has in common with another Stephanie you know?

Are they both redheads? If you do not know anyone with that name, perhaps you know of a story or a fictional character that has that same name. You can then picture them in that story and try to do it with as much detail as possible to create an effective marker.

Then, when you need to recall that their last name is Jones, you will remember the image of them wearing a hat and carrying a whip. Just like Indy did in *Raiders of the Lost Ark*.

If it is a foreign name or one you have never heard before, you should use the same technique that we used for learning new words. Any crazy example will work, and the more ludicrous or silly the example is, the more likely your memory will function when you call up the name. Sanjana, for example, is a pretty exotic name for most English speakers; but if you picture Sanjana sitting in the *sun* with your childhood friend *Jenna*, you have now linked her to different memories you have of Sun and memories you have of Jenna. Moreover, you will be very, very likely to remember her name when she approaches you at a cocktail party.

HOMEWORK

Check the Syllabus for homework assignments and recommended supplementary materials.

CHAPTER 37: SUPERLEARNING BY VIDEO OR AUDIO

As the final portion of this course, I want to talk about SuperLearning and speed learning using video. If you enjoy learning via video currently, that might actually change as you find that it is must faster for you to read new information. However, there are certain things that you would love or need to consume in video.

I, for example, love *TED* Talks. If I just read the captions, I am not going to get many visuals. What you can do in this case is a couple different things. One, you can join the *YouTube* HTML5 trial. This is their new technology, but it is a little bit buggy, and it does not quite work well.

I will give you the link in the Syllabus. It is a great free option. Unfortunately, this does not work for *YouTube* videos that are past a certain age, it does not work for *Vimeo*, and it does not work for online classes like *Udemy*. In that case, what you should go with is an app called MySpeed from Enounce. It works for Windows and Mac.

It is a little bit expensive at $30, but it allows you to speed up any video, flash, or HTML5 using keyboard shortcuts. You can hit faster, faster, faster, or you can hit your preferred speed. I personally choose to watch videos at 2x speed.

Of course, any time you learn anything, whether in a book, a conversation, or a video, you now know that you must make markers. You will notice that because you are used to creating markers so quickly during your reading, you will be able to make markers much faster during videos, too.

Honestly, it will almost drive you nuts if you watch lectures at a normal speed. Both Lev and I experienced this side effect after taking on this course, because we are so used to the "fire hose" of information.

Also, remember: when you are watching online videos, you still need to do your retrieval. You need to stop after ten minutes of a lecture and process, think about the markers you have created, store them, link them together, and create as much detail as possible.

This is *not* the time to abandon all the habits you have learned. Nor is it the time or forget all the important skills you have developed. It is just a matter of adapting them and creating the markers while watching a video instead of while reading

HOMEWORK

Check the Syllabus for homework assignments and recommended supplementary materials.

Chapter 38: Thank You & Congratulations

We have concluded the course. I want to thank you very, very much for participating in the course. Please share your new skills with your friends and family and give them the opportunity to experience the pleasure of SuperLearning.

You will notice that it is frustrating if you are reading a new book every few days and you want to share that book, story, or article with your friends, and they always tell you, "I will read it when I have time." I used to be that kind of person and now, I share this course with as many people as I possibly can.

I truly believe that if we can all learn to speed read and learn much faster, it is going to decrease the boundaries to learning new information. Anything is possible with information and knowledge.

I really hope you enjoyed the course. I hope you will share it. I hope you will give us feedback so we can constantly improve the course. Please reach out to us via the *Facebook* group if you have any questions or difficulties throughout the course. Thanks so much, and enjoy the journey.

Homework

Check the Syllabus for homework assignments and recommended supplementary materials.

That's it! You did it! Just remember; your skills will grow and develop the more you practice them. Never stop!

APPENDICES

APPENDIX 1: BASELINE READING SPEED AND RETENTION TEST 1

In order to understand and measure your progress in both reading speed and quality of retention, let's assess your baseline reading speed and comprehension.

Question 1:

Instructions:
Read the following text at the fastest speed you can, while attempting to remember and store at least 80% of the pertinent details. Use a timer, starting and stopping at the indicated points, to measure your speed. Once you have completed reading the selection, you will be asked a series of questions that test your understanding and retention of the material.

Speech: Copyright Franklin Delano Roosevelt, 1941. View the full text here:

http://jle.vi/roosevelt

--START YOUR TIMER--

Mr. Vice President, Mr. Speaker, Members of the Senate, and of the House of Representatives:

Yesterday, December 7th, 1941 -- a date which will live in infamy -- the United States of America was suddenly and deliberately attacked by naval and air forces of the Empire of Japan.

The United States was at peace with that nation and, at the solicitation of Japan, was still in conversation with its government and its emperor looking toward the maintenance of peace in the Pacific.

Indeed, one hour after Japanese air squadrons had commenced bombing in the American island of Oahu, the Japanese ambassador to the United States and his colleague delivered to our Secretary of State a formal reply to a recent American message. And while this reply stated that it seemed useless to continue the existing diplomatic negotiations, it contained no threat or hint of war or of armed attack.

It will be recorded that the distance of Hawaii from Japan makes it obvious that the attack was deliberately planned many days or even weeks ago. During the intervening time, the Japanese government has deliberately sought to deceive the United States by false statements and expressions of hope for continued peace.

The attack yesterday on the Hawaiian islands has caused severe damage to American naval and military forces. I regret to tell you that very many American lives have been lost. In addition, American ships have been reported torpedoed on the high seas between San Francisco and Honolulu.

Yesterday, the Japanese government also launched an attack against Malaya.

Last night, Japanese forces attacked Hong Kong.

Last night, Japanese forces attacked Guam.

Last night, Japanese forces attacked the Philippine Islands.

Last night, the Japanese attacked Wake Island.

And this morning, the Japanese attacked Midway Island.

Japan has, therefore, undertaken a surprise offensive extending throughout the Pacific area. The facts of yesterday and today speak for themselves. The people of the United States have already formed their opinions and well understand the implications to the very life and safety of our nation.

As Commander in Chief of the Army and Navy, I have directed that all measures be taken for our defense. But always will our whole nation remember the character of the onslaught against us.

No matter how long it may take us to overcome this premeditated invasion, the American people in their righteous might will win through to absolute victory.

I believe that I interpret the will of the Congress and of the people when I assert that we will not only defend ourselves to the uttermost, but will make it very certain that this form of treachery shall never again endanger us.

Hostilities exist. There is no blinking at the fact that our people, our territory, and our interests are in grave danger.

With confidence in our armed forces, with the unbounding determination of our people, we will gain the inevitable triumph -- so help us God.

I ask that the Congress declare that since the unprovoked and dastardly attack by Japan on Sunday, December 7th, 1941, a state of war has existed between the United States and the Japanese empire.

--STOP YOUR TIMER--

How long did it take you to read this text (518 words) with ≥ 80% retention?

- Under 1 Minute (Over 500 words per minute)
- 1:00 - 1:30 (300-500 words per minute)
- 1:30 - 2:00 (250-300 words per minute)
- 2:00 - 2:30 (200-250 words per minute)
- 2:30 - 3:00 (175-200 words per minute)
- Over 3 Minutes (Less than 150 words per minute)

(To get an exact number, divide 518 by the number of seconds on your timer, then multiple by 60. For example, if it took you 2 minutes 20 seconds, you would divide 518 by 140 seconds and multiply by 60, for a result of 222 words per minute.)

○ Reading Speed: _____wpm

Question 2:
   What day was the speech delivered?
   • December 7, 1941
   • December 1, 1941
   • December 8, 1941
   • December 9, 1941

Question 3:
   The Japanese failed to reply to the message sent by the United States.
   • True
   • False

Question 4:
   Which of the following had **not** been attacked by Japanese Forces at the time of the speech?
   • Hong Kong
   • Guam
   • Wake Island
   • Midway Island
   • Marshall Islands
   • Oahu
   • Philippine Islands

Question 5:
   In addition to the land attacks, US ships between San Francisco and Honolulu were targeted in which type of attacks?
   • Kamikaze
   • Fire bombing
   • Torpedo
   • Cannon

Question 6:
   The speaker is delivering his speech in his capacity as:
   • Commander of the Navy

- The President of the United States
- The Secretary of Defense
- The Commander in Chief of the Army and Navy

Question 7:
   The speaker describes the acts of the Japanese forces as "unspeakable."
- True
- False

Question 8:
   Which phrase does the speaker **not** mention in his speech?
- Japanese Ambassador
- Secretary of State
- Pearl Harbor
- Washington, D.C.
- Mr. Vice President
- Malaya

Answers

1. Reading Speed: _____wpm

    Reading Retention: _____%

2. December 8, 1941

3. False

4. Marshall Islands

5. Torpedo

6. The Commander in Chief of the Army and Navy

7. False

8. Pearl Harbor

APPENDIX 2: READING SPEED AND RETENTION TEST 2

We have yet to get into speed reading itself, but by now, your comprehension should have improved dramatically, and with the skill of pre-reading, you should be able to read a little bit faster.

Check your progress with this quick speed and comprehension test.

If you do not see a major improvement in your speed, don't worry: that is coming up in this chapter. You should however see a marked difference in your retention score.

Question 1

Instructions:

Read the following text at the fastest speed you can, while attempting to remember and store at least 80% of the pertinent details. Use a timer, starting and stopping at the indicated points, to measure your speed. Once you have completed this question, you will be asked a series of questions that test your understanding and retention of the material.

--START YOUR TIMER--

Ladies and Gentlemen,

I'm only going to talk to you just for a minute or so this evening, because I have some -- some very sad news for all of you -- Could you lower those signs, please? -- I have some very sad news for all of you, and, I think, sad news for all of our fellow citizens, and people who love peace all over the world; and that is that Martin Luther King was shot and was killed tonight in Memphis, Tennessee.

Martin Luther King dedicated his life to love and to justice between fellow human beings. He died in the cause of that effort. In this difficult day, in this difficult time for the United States, it's perhaps well to ask what kind of a nation we are and what direction we want to move in. For those of you who are black -- considering the evidence evidently is that there were white people who were responsible -- you can be filled with bitterness, and with hatred, and a desire for revenge.

We can move in that direction as a country, in greater polarization -- black people amongst blacks, and white amongst whites, filled with hatred toward one another. Or we can make an effort, as Martin Luther King did, to understand, and to comprehend, and replace that violence, that stain of bloodshed that has spread across our land, with an effort to understand, compassion, and love.

For those of you who are black and are tempted to fill with -- be filled with hatred and mistrust of the injustice of such an act, against all white people, I would only say that I can also feel in my own heart the same kind of feeling. I had a member of my family killed, but he was killed by a white man.

But we have to make an effort in the United States. We have to make an effort to understand, to get beyond, or go beyond these rather difficult times.

My favorite poem, my -- my favorite poet was Aeschylus. And he once wrote:

Even in our sleep, pain which cannot forget
falls drop by drop upon the heart,
until, in our own despair,
against our will,
comes wisdom
through the awful grace of God.

What we need in the United States is not division; what we need in the United States is not hatred; what we need in the United States is not violence and lawlessness, but is love, and wisdom, and compassion toward one another, and a feeling of justice toward those who still suffer within our country, whether they be white or whether they be black.

So I ask you tonight to return home, to say a prayer for the family of Martin Luther King -- yeah, it's true -- but more importantly to say a prayer for our own country, which all of us love -- a prayer for understanding and that compassion of which I spoke.

We can do well in this country. We will have difficult times. We've had difficult times in the past, but we -- and we will have difficult times in the future. It is not the end of violence; it is not the end of lawlessness; and it's not the end of disorder.

But the vast majority of white people and the vast majority of black people in this country want to live together, want to improve the quality of our life, and want justice for all human beings that abide in our land.

And let's dedicate ourselves to what the Greeks wrote so many years ago: to tame the savageness of man and make gentle the life of this world. Let us dedicate ourselves to that, and say a prayer for our country and for our people.

Thank you very much.

--STOP YOUR TIMER--

How long did it take you to read this text (625 words) with ≥ 80% retention?

- Under 1 Minute (Over 600 words per minute)
- 1:00 - 1:30 (400-600 words per minute)
- 1:30 - 2:00 (300-400 words per minute)
- 2:00 - 2:30 (250-300 words per minute)
- 2:30 - 3:00 (200-250 words per minute)
- Over 3 Minutes (Less than 200 words per minute)

(To get an exact number, divide 625 by the number of seconds on your timer, then multiple by 60. For example, if it took you 2 minutes 20 seconds, you would divide 625 by 140 seconds and multiply by 60, for a result of 268 words per minute.)

This speech is copyrighted material. View the original:

http://www.americanrhetoric.com/speeches/rfkon mlkdeath.htm

Question 2
   Martin Luther King was shot and killed in
   • Memphis, Tennessee
   • Nashville, Tennessee
   • Jacksonville, Florida
   • Birmingham, Alabama

Question 3
   The speaker gives his audience a choice between moving forward with greater polarization or making an effort to replace violence with understanding, compassion, and love.
   • True
   • False

Question 4
   The speaker mentions that a member of his own family was also killed.
   • True
   • False

Question 5
   The speaker shares his favorite poem, a work by the poet...
   • Homer
   • Aeschylus
   • Socrates
   • Robert Frost

Question 6
   The speaker lists various things that the United States does not need. Which of these does he **not** mention?
   • Division
   • Hatred

- Violence
- Segregation
- Lawlessness

Question 7
Which of the following does the speaker urge the audience to pray for?
- The family if Martin Luther King
- Their own country
- Understanding
- Compassion
- All of the above

Question 8
The speaker remembered to thank his audience at the end of his speech.
- True
- False

Answers to Test 2

1. Reading Speed: _____wpm

   Reading Retention: _____%

2. Memphis, Tennessee

3. True

4. True

5. Aeschylus

6. Segregation

7. All of the above

8. True

APPENDIX 3: READING SPEED AND RETENTION TEST 3

Take this quiz only after you have been practicing your optimized, efficient saccades and broken the "sound barrier." This should take a couple of weeks, so we recommend skipping the quiz for now if you intend to continue reading. Come back to it later to track your progress!

Question 1

Instructions:
Read the following text at the fastest speed you can, while attempting to remember and store at least 80% of the pertinent details. Use a timer, starting and stopping at the indicated points, to measure your speed. Once you have completed this question, you will be asked a series of questions that test your understanding and retention of the material.

--START YOUR TIMER--

I am honored to be with you today at your commencement from one of the finest universities in the world. I never graduated from college. Truth be told, this is the closest I've ever gotten to a college graduation. Today I want to tell you three stories from my life. That is it. No big deal. Just three stories.

The first story is about connecting the dots.

I dropped out of Reed College after the first 6 months, but then stayed around as a drop-in for another 18 months or so before I really quit. So why did I drop out?

It started before I was born. My biological mother was a young, unwed college graduate student, and she decided to put me up for adoption. She felt very strongly that I should be adopted by college graduates, so everything was all set for me to be adopted at birth by a lawyer and his wife. Except that when I popped out they decided at the last minute that they really wanted a girl. So my parents, who were on a waiting list, got a call in the middle of the night asking: "We have an unexpected baby boy; do you want him?" They said: "Of course." My biological mother later found out that my mother had never graduated from college and that my father had never graduated from high school. She refused to sign the final adoption papers. She only relented a few months later when my parents promised that I would someday go to college.

And 17 years later I did go to college. But I naively chose a college that was almost as expensive as Stanford, and all of my working-class parents' savings were being spent on my college tuition. After six months, I couldn't see the value in it. I had no idea what I wanted to do with my life and no idea how college was going to help me figure it out. And here I was spending all of the money my parents had saved their entire life. So I decided to drop out and trust that it would all work out OK. It was pretty scary at the time, but looking back it was one of the best decisions I ever made. The minute I dropped out I could stop taking the required classes that didn't interest me, and begin dropping in on the ones that looked interesting.

It wasn't all romantic. I didn't have a dorm room, so I slept on the floor in friends' rooms, I returned coke bottles for the 5¢ deposits to buy food with, and I would walk the 7 miles across town every Sunday night to get one good meal a week at the Hare Krishna temple. I loved it. And much of what I stumbled into by following my curiosity and intuition turned out to be priceless later on. Let me give you one example:

Reed College at that time offered perhaps the best calligraphy instruction in the country. Throughout the campus every poster, every label on every drawer, was beautifully hand calligraphed. Because I had dropped out and didn't have to take the normal classes, I decided to take a calligraphy class to learn how to do this.

I learned about serif and san serif typefaces, about varying the amount of space between different letter combinations, about what makes great typography great. It was beautiful, historical, artistically subtle in a way that science can't capture, and I found it fascinating...

--STOP YOUR TIMER--

How long did it take you to read this text (625 words) with ≥ 80% retention?
- Under 1 Minute (Over 600 words per minute)
- 1:00 - 1:30 (400-600 words per minute)
- 1:30 - 2:00 (300-400 words per minute)
- 2:00 - 2:30 (250-300 words per minute)
- 2:30 - 3:00 (200-250 words per minute)
- Over 3 Minutes (Less than 200 words per minute)

(To get an exact number, divide 584 by the number of seconds on your timer, then multiple by 60. For example, if it took you 2 minutes 20 seconds, you would divide 584 by 49 seconds and multiply by 60, for a result of 715 words per minute.)

This speech is copyrighted; view the original:

http://jle.vi/sj

I have measured and recorded my speed alongside my previous measurement - now test my comprehension!

Question 2
    The speaker tells us he never...
- Graduated from college
- Attended college
- Understood why people go to college
- Regretted dropping out of college

Question 3
    The speaker dropped out of _____ College after the first _____ months, but he stayed around for another 18 months or so.

Question 4
    The speaker's biological parents gave him up because they wanted a girl.
- True
- False

Question 5
    The speaker's biological mother insisted all of the following **except** that...
- Her child be adopted by college graduates
- Her child go to college
- Her child would grow up with siblings

Question 6
    The speaker dropped out of college because...
- It was too expensive for his parents
- He didn't see the value in it
- He didn't know what he wanted to do in life
- He figured it would work out "OK"
- All of the above

Question 7
    Which of the following did the speaker **not** do to get by after dropping out of college?
- Return Coke bottles
- Sleep on the floor
- Walk long distances
- Eat at a Hare Krishna Temple
- Sell artwork

Question 8
The speaker tells the story of how he became fascinated with one subject in particular: _____

Answers
1. Reading Speed: _____wpm

    Reading Retention: _____%

2. Graduated from college

3. Reed, 6 months

4. False

5. Her child would grow up with siblings

6. All of the above

7. Sell artwork

8. Calligraphy

APPENDIX 4: WE WOULD LOVE TO HEAR FROM YOU!

If you have questions, comments, concerns, or any other type of inquiry, please reach out to us:

superlearner@jle.vi

GLOSSARY

Encoding – adding meaning to the information by converting it into something we understand: acoustic, semantic (meaning), or visual information.

Gordian knot: The Gordian Knot is a legend of Phrygian Gordium associated with Alexander the Great. It is often used as a metaphor for an intractable problem (disentangling an "impossible" knot) solved easily by cheating or "thinking outside the box" ("cutting the Gordian knot").

Life Hacking: Refers to any trick, shortcut, skill, or novelty method that increases productivity and efficiency, in all walks of life. It is arguably a modern appropriation of a Gordian knot - in other words, anything that solves an everyday problem in an inspired, ingenious manner

Marker: Mental images that have been created and imbued with details, which are used to represent specific information

Neurons: Electrically excitable cells that transmit information using electrochemical signals

Polyglot (noun): A person who speaks, writes, or reads a number of languages

Retrieval –accessing the newly-stored information, thereby solidifying its neural connections and integrity

Saccade (noun): A rapid movement of the eye between fixation points

Storage – transferring the encoded information from working memory to short term memory and (hopefully) to long term memory

SuperLearner (noun): One who is repeatedly able to synthesize, understand, and retain vast amounts of information in abnormally short periods of time. A SuperLearner is a person who desires to take learning to the next level by acquiring skills that enhance reading speed, comprehension, and memory

Synapse: These electrically excitable cells process and transmit information using electrochemical signals. These signals are called synapses. Synapses are specialized connections between the cells.

ABOUT THE AUTHORS

JONATHAN A. LEVI SUPERLEARNER (800+WPM), LIFE HACKER, ENTREPRENEUR, INVESTOR

Jonathan Levi is an experienced entrepreneur, angel investor, and lifehacker from Silicon Valley.

After successfully selling his Inc 5,000 rated startup in April of 2011, Levi packed up for Israel to gain experience in the Venture Capital industry. While in Israel, Levi enlisted the help of speed-reading expert and university professor Anna Goldentouch and machine learning expert Dr. Lev Goldentouch, who tutored him in speed-reading, advanced memorization, and more. Levi saw incredible results while earning his MBA from INSEAD, and was overwhelmed with the amount of interest his classmates expressed in acquiring the same skill set. Since acquiring this "SuperLearning" skill, he has become a proficient lifehacker, optimizing and "hacking" such processes as travel, sleep, language learning, and fitness. He later collaborated with his tutors, creating the blockbuster *Udemy* course *Become a SuperLearner* among others. More recently, he has founded the *Becoming SuperHuman Blog & Podcast*, a spinoff brand of his successful online courses.

Levi has been featured in such publications and programs as the *Wall Street Journal, Nana10 Television, The Silicon Valley Business Journal, Bimmer Magazine, BMW Blog*, and Donna Fenn's latest book, *Upstarts! How GenY Entrepreneurs are Rocking the World of Business and 8 Ways You Can Profit from Their Success*, among other blogs, podcasts, and publications.

Dr. Lev Goldentouch, Lifehacker And Technology Guru

Dr. Lev Goldentouch earned his PhD in machine learning and information theory when he was 27 years old. Understanding the similarities of machine learning and human super-learning allowed Lev to learn immense amounts of knowledge in many technological and cognitive subjects. Immediately afterwards Lev opened a consulting company, which offers its services to highly skilled individuals, agile startups and technological giants like Samsung.

The super-learning tools developed by Lev allow ordinary people to learn at 10 times the speed of their colleagues, and enable machines to solve extremely complex problems.

Lev is an active lifehacker, holds a number of patents, and is constantly looking for new and better ways to do things. He takes great pride in sharing his unique knowledge and experience with others.

Lev is also a prolific writer. Lev published several books and articles on various technical and cognitive subjects, creativity and languages. Lev's blog www.keytostudy.com holds a large number of insightful advices, training exercises and useful resources.

Prof. Anna Goldentouch, Education Guru

Prof. Anna Goldentouch started teaching super-learning skills when she was 17 years old. Anna developed the super-learning abilities as a tool to deal with personal dyslexia, after taking several courses on super-learning. After finishing advanced degrees in education and sociology, Anna started to teach in Bar Ilan and Ben Gurion Universities in Israel. Anna's courses on speed reading, memory development and didactic techniques are extremely popular with students. Anna also provides consulting services and training for various large companies and government services.

Anna made it her mission to teach people how to learn in a better, more efficient and fulfilling way.

Anna provides 1:1 Skype sessions for students all over the world, seminars for institutions, corporate bodies and government organizations. Anna's ability to create extremely effective custom-tailored learning strategies saved countless hours to tens of thousands on Anna's students. Anyone in need of Anna's advice can write to info@keytostudy.com

OTHER BOOKS AND COURSES

Become a SuperLearner: Learn Advanced Memory & Speed Reading (90% Off): http://jle.vi/1j

Become a Speed Demon: Automation & Efficiency to Reclaim Time (90% Off): http://jle.vi/1k

Become a Travel Wizard: Lean to Game the System & Travel for Free (90% Off): http://jle.vi/1l

Made in the USA
San Bernardino, CA
02 April 2015